YORKSHIRE GREATS

Yorkshire Greats

The county's fifty finest

Bernard Ingham

Dalesman

First published in 2005 by Dalesman
an imprint of
Country Publications Ltd
The Water Mill
Broughton Hall
Skipton
North Yorkshire
BD23 3AG

First edition 2005

Text © Bernard Ingham 2005
Illustrations © copyright holders 2005

A British Library Cataloguing-in-Publication record is available for this book

ISBN 1 85568 220 6

Repro by PPS Grasmere, Leeds
Printed by Compass Press, China

Contents

Introduction

This is the most dangerous book I shall ever write. Identifying the greatest men and women of any English county is more or less guaranteed to cause profound angst. But to proclaim the fifty greatest Yorkshire men and women — that is, those born within the ancient county — is tempting fate. After all, Yorkshiremen are 'aggressive, argumentative, intolerant and just plain down-right bloody-minded', in the words of the late Don Mosey, BBC cricket commentator and Dalesman. Yorkshire women are even fiercer. Both have decided views that they are not inclined to keep to themselves when they believe an injustice has been done.

I shall face some very fast bowling for leaving out Geoffrey Boycott, Hedley Verity, Ray Illingworth and Herbert Sutcliffe, to mention only a few cricketers. I shall be summarily shot for ignoring the claims of Dickie Bird, the Barnsley character who was once the world's most famous cricket umpire. I shall be dismissed as blind as the average (expletive deleted) referee by soccer fans for not finding a place for Wilf Mannion, Don Revie, Kevin Keegan, Gordon Banks and David Seaman. And no Jeff Butterfield (rugby union), not a single mention of a rugby league great, no Harvey Smith, the Bingley horseman, no Beryl Burton, cyclist extraordinaire, and no Anita Lonsborough, the Olympic swimming gold medallist. And that's only sport. Just wait, Ingham, when the modern entertainment industry finds itself ignored. You're for the high jump. Then there are the devotees of every other facet of human activity who will be sorely aggrieved over my choices and, being Yorkshire folk, will say so bluntly.

I told you this book was dangerous. I recognised this even at the moment of its conception in the disarming atmosphere of the Dalesman's offices in the Water Mill, Broughton Hall, Skipton. Everything always seems all right with the world in that idyllic corner of Yorkshire. It seemed even rosier when I was presented with the lists of Yorkshire Greats that the *Dalesman*'s readers have compiled over the years. It would have remained tolerably simple, if still dangerous, had I relied upon that gathering of Yorkshire thoughts and whittled the candidates down to fifty. But, haunted by the possibility that, even with the benefit of this collective cudgelling of the best brains on the subject, I might leave an awful gap that would destroy the book's credibility, I reached for the dictionaries of birthplaces and biographies. On a memorable cruise to Peru I combed through the 1,020 pages of the *Cambridge Dictionary of Biography* and came up with 226 distinguished Yorkshire persons. I was spoiled for choice with two kings, three Prime Ministers, two Speakers of the Commons, three Poets Laureate and seven Nobel Prize winners. Things had got out of hand.

The list would have been even longer had I taken risks with the definition of a Yorkshireman now ignored by Yorkshire County Cricket Club. My rigorous insistence on candidates being born beyond peradventure on Yorkshire soil rules out Caedmon, Whitby Abbey's herdsman-poet of the Dark Ages, and a whole celebration of saints — Hilda (Whitby), Wilfrid (Ripon), and Cedd and his brother Chad (Lastingham). We simply don't know where they came into this world. For the same reason, Cartimandua, the Brigantian collaborator who betrayed Caractacus to the Romans, escapes inclusion as an arch-villainess. Nor am I going to come between MPs in Yorkshire and Nottinghamshire who are fratching over whether Robin Hood was a Yorkshire or Nottinghamshire man. Nothing would please me more than to proclaim Robin Hood a Tyke. But where's the proof? Others must remain honorary Yorkshire folk, such as the distinguished Labour politicians, Denis Healey (born Mattingley, Hants) and Barbara Castle (Chesterfield).

So, before you stick pins in my effigy for ignoring your candidate, please make sure that he or she first had their bottom slapped by a midwife in one of the old Ridings.

This inflexible rule helped to keep the number of candidates down. But it does not reduce it enough. Only a tight prescription of what it is to be a Yorkshire Great can do that. I have been guided by an individual's established reputation, recognised stature, character, international impact and contribution to the human race, especially when it was made against the odds or in the face of prejudice such as experienced by John Harrison, the inventor of the marine chronometer to fix longitude, and Brian Clough, the football manager.

Inevitably, my guideline inclines to historical rather than contemporary figures, if only because we can better see their contribution to human development. The modern cult of the television celebrity also tends to handicap a living candidate. Too many of them are here today and gone tomorrow. Unlike old soldiers, they don't just fade away; they evaporate. On this basis a contemporary figure has to be truly great to become a Yorkshire Great. Let us therefore salute Dame Janet Baker, the opera singer from Hatfield; John Barry, composer of film scores from York; Alan Bennett, actor and playwright from Leeds; Baroness Betty Boothroyd, former Speaker of the House of Commons from Dewsbury; Alan Hinkes, the mountaineer from Northallerton; David Hockney, the artist from Bradford; and not least Freddie Trueman, the legendary cricketer from Stainton, South Yorkshire.

Some choices are frankly invidious. How, for example, do you choose between the forty-six Yorkshire winners of the Victoria Cross or the smaller number of holders of its civilian equivalent, the George Cross? The only way is to advance a representative of the gallant. I fear I may have ill-used the Yorkshire miner in not selecting one of their number to represent GCs. Most of the GCs awarded to *prima facie* Yorkshire folk have gone to miners for heroism in assorted tragedies underground — no fewer than six in one incident at Bentley Colliery in 1931. But GC records, unlike those of VCs, are virtually useless on birthplaces.

As for Nobel Prize winners, I confess to a rank prejudice in favour of Sir John Cockcroft, the atom splitter, from Todmorden in my native upper Calder Valley. He presented me with my shorthand prize at Todmorden Technical College in the late 1940s. He is, in fact, one of three Nobel prize winners from upper Calder Valley. The others are the late Sir Geoffrey Wilkinson, the inorganic chemist, also, believe it or not, from Todmorden, and John E Walker, the biochemist from Halifax. Fancy, three Nobel men in a twelve-mile stretch of a single Pennine valley.

I explain the reason for my selection of each Great at the beginning of their entry. In the interests of reducing Yorkshire blood pressure, I should perhaps explain over whom I have sucked my teeth, beaten my breast and kicked the wall. Exploration is so dominated by Captain James Cook (Marton-in-Cleveland) that Sir Martin Frobisher (Altofts), the Rev William Scoresby

(Cropton, near Whitby) and Sir Douglas Mawson, the geologist from Shipley, tend to be overlooked. Similarly, Harrison overshadows a whole clutch of inventors — Joseph Aspdin (Portland cement) from Leeds; Sir Donald Bailey (Bailey bridge) from Rotherham; Samuel Cunliffe Lister, Baron Masham (textile machinery) from Bradford; and Joseph Aloysius Hansom (horse-drawn cab) from York. It grieves me, given Yorkshire's reputation for tightfistedness, not to have found a place for philanthropists such as Seebohm Rowntree (York), Sir Francis Crossley (Halifax) or Lady Sue Ryder (Leeds). I also pondered on the claims of Roger Ascham, the humanist and scholar from Kirby Wiske; Phil May, the caricaturist from Wortley, Leeds; W H Auden, the poet from York; and Helen Sharman, the first British astronaut from Sheffield.

If it helps the film and theatre world, I did not ignore Tom Courtenay (Hull), Ben Kingsley (Snainton), James Mason (Huddersfield) and most certainly not Dame Judi Dench (York); or, in the case of entertainment, Maureen Lipman (Hull), Dame Diana Rigg (Doncaster), Sir Brian Rix (Cottingham), Michael Palin (Sheffield) or Michael Parkinson (Barnsley).

It is as well you should know I also looked at such distinguished people as Professor Jocelyn Bell Burnell, the astronomer and discoverer of the first pulsars (York); George Birkbeck, founder of the Mechanics' Institutes (Settle); Simon Marks, the architect if not the founder of Marks and Spencer (Leeds); and such medical luminaries as Henry Maudsley (Giggleswick) and John Radcliffe (Wakefield). I would dearly have loved to include Wilfred Rhodes (Kirkheaton), the greatest all-rounder of them all, who was recalled to the England cricket team at the age of fifty-two.

By now you will realise that I sweated blood writing this book. I hope you will not be after more of it when you have read it. In these pages you will discover one undeniable truth about Yorkshire Greats: they were invariably born with that awkward gene that is characteristic of Yorkshire species. The DNA of Captain Cook, William Wilberforce and John Harrison, my three Greatest of the Great, was richly endowed with that gritty determination, that wilful refusal to give up and that sheer bloody-mindedness that eventually prevails. So, much more modestly, is mine. Hence this act of homage.

Captain James Cook

1728-79

The greatest explorer — and greatest Yorkshireman — of them all, who opened up the world in tiny Whitby colliers scarcely 100 feet long.

He peacefully changed the map of the world more than any other man in history. He set new standards in seamanship, navigation, cartography, the health of his crews, relations with natives and in discovery. His name is perpetuated in inlet, island, strait and mountain from Alaska to New Zealand. And he did it all in Whitby 'cats', sturdy but tiny flat-bottomed coal ships in which he

facing page A three-quarter-length portrait of Captain James Cook by Nathaniel Dance. He is wearing a captain's full-dress uniform, and is pointing to the east coast of Australia on his own chart of the Southern Ocean. Cook sat for this portrait 'for a few hours before dinner' on the 25th May 1776, before he left on his third voyage, never to return. David Samwell, surgeon on the *Discovery*, thought it 'a most excellent likeness … and … the only one I have seen that bears any resemblance to him'. *(© National Maritime Museum, London, Greenwich Hospital Collection.)*

right Captain Cook's birthplace. Built in 1755 in the village of Great Ayton by his parents, in 1934 it was shipped to and re-erected in Fitzroy Gardens, Melbourne, Australia. *(Rex Features.)*

CAPTAIN JAMES COOK

11

learned his mariner's trade. Captain James Cook, the greatest explorer in the history of the planet, was and remains the towering figure among Yorkshiremen.

Born the second of eight children of a farm labourer at Marton-in-Cleveland, when Cook was eight his father moved a few miles to Great Ayton to manage a farm for Thomas Skottowe. The estate owner paid a penny a week for James, a robust loner, to be educated locally where the Cook Schoolroom Museum now stands. In spite of his aptitude for sums, he joined his father on the farm at twelve and then five years later became shop boy for William Sanderson, a grocer and draper in the fishing village of Staithes fifteen miles away. The sea entered his soul.

A year later Sanderson found the tall, fair and serious young man an apprenticeship with the Walker brothers, Quaker ship-owners at Whitby. He learned his seamanship plying up and down the East Coast and across the

facing page The replica of Captain Cook's ship *Endeavour* enters Whitby harbour during its 2004 voyage. *(Photo by Mike Kipling.)*

below Map from the *Complete History of Captain Cook's First, Second and Third Voyages* (1784) showing Cook's three Pacific voyages. The first voyage was to observe the transit of Venus and to seek out the fifth continent — Australia. The second and third voyages further explored the Pacific, and sought a northern sea passage between the Pacific and Atlantic oceans. *(Science Museum Library.)*

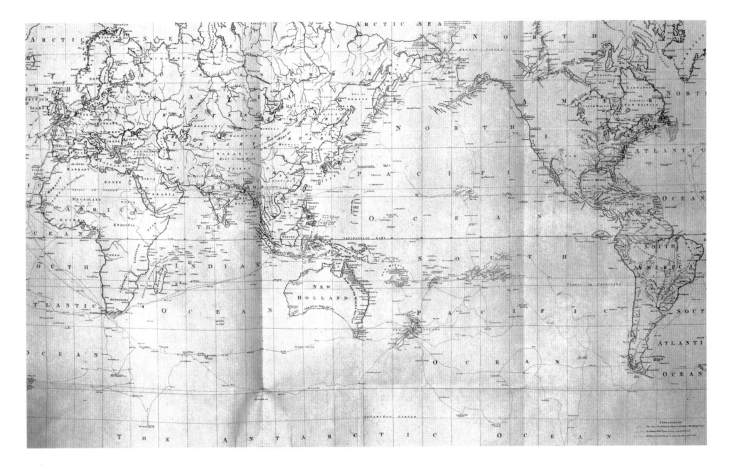

North Sea. Within eight years the Walkers offered him a mastership but he turned them down to 'try his fortune' in 1755 in the Royal Navy, then described by an admiral as 'manned by violence and maintained by cruelty'.

In less than a month he was master's mate on the grossly undermanned HMS *Eagle*, patrolling the Western Approaches during the Seven Years War with France, and was given command of a captured ship. He got his master's certificate, with full responsibility for navigation under a captain, within two years, and in 1758 sailed with the fleet for Canada as master of HMS *Pembroke*, a new sixty-four gunner. His charting of the St Lawrence River contributed to the success of General Wolfe's landing. For five years after the war

The discovery of Terra Australis: Captain James Cook raises the Union Jack flag on a beach in Australia. An illustration from an oil painting by Algernon Talmadge. *(Photo by Hulton Archive/Getty Images.)*

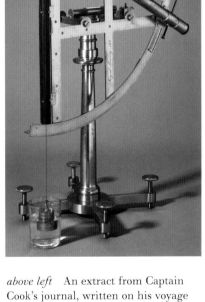

(1763-8), commanding the schooner *Grenville* in Newfoundland, he built up a formidable reputation as a surveyor.

He was hastily commissioned in 1768 when the Royal Society and the Admiralty organised the first scientific expedition to the Pacific. He sailed in this, the first of his three epic voyages, in a 368-ton ninety-eight foot long Whitby collier, renamed the *Endeavour*.

He was ordered to take scientists to Tahiti to observe the transit of Venus across the sun and then find Terra Australis, the so-called southern continent that philosophers argued must exist to balance the Northern Hemisphere's landmass. Cook found and then over six months charted New Zealand, surveyed the eastern coast of Australia and navigated the Great Barrier Reef after being temporarily stuck on it, returning home via Batavia (Jakarta) and the Cape of Good Hope. His call in pestilential Batavia cost him thirty men to disease and fever — a horrible blow since his strict regime of cleanliness, ventilation and sauerkraut made him a Royal Navy byword for scurvy-free ships.

He was promoted to commander, presented to George III and promptly dispatched in another Whitby 'cat', *Resolution* — accompanied by the *Adventure*

above left An extract from Captain Cook's journal, written on his voyage to the South Pole and round the world. *(Photo by Folb/Topical Press Agency/ Getty Images.)*

above This portable astronomical quadrant was made in London by the famous instrument-maker John Bird. It was sent with one of the expeditions dispatched by the Royal Society to measure the 1769 transit of Venus. Captain Cook, who observed the event from Tahiti on his first voyage to the South Pacific, may have even used this particular instrument. An astronomical quadrant was employed to measure the angle of a celestial object from the zenith. Objects were sighted using a pivoting telescope fitted with a crosshair wire. *(Science Museum.)*

— on an even more ambitious expedition. His task was to circumnavigate and penetrate Antarctica with his quota of scientists who had brought back much new knowledge from his first voyage. Between 1772-5 he proved there was no Terra Australis, except what might lie beyond the ice shelf, penetrating down to 70° south; made the first high-latitude west-east circumnavigation of Antarctica; charted Tonga and Easter Island; and discovered New Caledonia, the South Sandwich Islands and South Georgia — and lost not a single man to scurvy.

He was at last promoted to captain and elected a Fellow of the Royal Society. One challenge remained: the elusive Northwest Passage via the Bering Strait between Alaska and Russia. In the *Resolution*, with a certain budding Captain Bligh on board, accompanied by another Whitby ship, the *Discovery*, he found no way through. Ironically, given his normally good relations with them, he was killed by natives on the beach at Kealakekua Bay in Hawaii in a dispute over the theft of a boat. The *Gazette* reported that the king shed tears at the news and ordered a £300-a-year pension for his widow.

English explorer Captain James Cook witnesses a human sacrifice in Tahiti in 1769. *(Photo by Hulton Archive/ Getty Images.)*

Cook's endurance was matched by that of his wife, daughter of a boarding house keeper in London's dockland, whom he married when he was thirty. He was at sea for more than half their married life and three of their children died in infancy. His widow spent the last forty-one years of her life mourning her husband and another three sons, two of whom joined the Royal Navy, who died young.

An unfinished painting by Johann Zoffany *circa* 1795 showing the death of Captain James Cook, at Kealakekua Bay, Hawaii, on the 14th February 1779 during his third Pacific voyage. *(© National Maritime Museum, London, Greenwich Hospital Collection.)*

William Wilberforce

1759-1833

No man exercised more moral authority over the nation. He lived to see Britain abolish the slave trade and know that Parliament would outlaw slavery.

William Wilberforce is known as the man who ended the slave trade and even slavery. He did neither but he accomplished much more. He certainly brought about the abolition of the British slave trade in 1807 but others continued this 'detestable and guilty' traffic for decades after his death. Slavery persisted even longer, but he lived just long enough to know that the British Parliament would at last outlaw it.

William Wilberforce (played by John Mills, left) and Charles Fox (Robert Morley, centre) talk to the prime minister William Pitt (Robert Donat, right), in a scene from the 1941 film *Young Mr Pitt. (Photo by Bill Brandt/Picture Post/Getty Images.)*

William Wilberforce by George Richmond (watercolour, 1833). An evangelical Christian and social reformer, Wilberforce dedicated himself to the 'suppression of the Slave Trade and the reformation of manners'. He entered Parliament in 1780 as a Tory MP and was the Parliamentary leader of the abolition movement from 1787. After years of campaigning, Wilberforce's bill to end Britain's part in slave trading was passed to a standing ovation in 1807. A further act of 1833 provided for the emancipation of slaves in British colonies. *(Courtesy National Portrait Gallery, London.)*

Wilberforce House in Hull has been a museum since 1906. Each year, on the nearest weekday to 29th July, a ceremony is held in the city in his memory. *(Wilberforce House, Hull City Museums and Art Galleries.)*

This puny, ailing Hull man — five feet three inches in his socks and with a thirty-three inch chest — became 'the conscience of the nation' and, in the words of his biographer, John Pollock, 'secured personal moral authority with public and Parliament above any man living'. He is undoubtedly among the greatest of Great Yorkshiremen.

His family originated in Wilberfoss, near York, and had made its fortune in the Baltic trade. He was born into Hull's aristocracy and was briefly at Hull Grammar School before his father died when he was nine. He was then sent to live with a beloved uncle and aunt in Wimbledon until his mother dispatched him to Pocklington School to isolate him from, to her, the dangerous bug of Methodism.

Wilberforce had a quick mind, but was idle and was never encouraged to work at St John's College, Cambridge. Nor need he have done a stroke after Cambridge, such was his inheritance. But he was no rake in a debauched age. He began to dream of a life in politics and, together with Pitt the Younger, his

The actual wooden model of the slave ship Brookes *used by William Wilberforce in the House of Commons to demonstrate conditions on the so-called 'middle passage' of the slave trade.* (Wilberforce House, Hull City Museums and Art Galleries, UK; www.bridgeman.co.uk.)

AM I NOT A MAN & A BROTHER

close friend from Cambridge, he soaked up the Commons' atmosphere from the Strangers' Gallery.

He beat Pitt to a seat, securing the rotten borough of Hull for £8,000 when he was just twenty-one. Four years later he became for twenty-eight years one of the two most powerful MPs as a knight of the shire of Yorkshire. His success in entering Parliament in the face of the landed aristocracy speaks for his charisma, oratory and political nous. Boswell testified that 'this shrimp swelled into a whale' on the hustings.

Yet for all his abilities and connections — successive Prime Ministers treated him as an honorary privy councillor in the access they gave him to documents and information — he never held office. He was a true independent.

He showed an interest in slavery from the first as an MP, but it was not until he underwent 'a rebirth of the soul' to become an Evangelical Christian in 1785-6 that he emerged as a reformer. His overriding interest was the improvement of the slaves' condition in the West Indies, the state of Africa and the slave trade. To these ends he brought forward over more than twenty years umpteen motions and bills before and after the abolition of the British slave trade. His industry and perseverance — and ability to inspire disciples — was phenomenal.

This was only the most visible of his work. His chaotic, eccentric home — he married a rich girl at thirty-eight and had six children — became a clearing house for philanthropy and good causes. At one stage he was an official of sixty-nine different societies. His concerns ranged over the poor, racial and religious intolerance, criminal justice reform (especially capital punishment and prison conditions), boy chimney-sweeps, inoculation against smallpox, bull baiting (which led to the RSPCA), the Church Missionary Society, the British and Foreign Bible Society, and Church Missions to India.

For his pains he was cut by the king and vested interests, derided as St Wilberforce and cruelly accused of being more concerned for black slaves abroad than white wage slaves at home. William Cobbett rejoiced in his fugitive exile in America: 'Think of it — no Wilberforce'. The wonder was not that he attracted venom in a cruel, dissipated age beset by Napoleonic wars but that he achieved the moral regeneration of the nation.

He had weak eyesight, a tendency to colitis, eventually curvature of the spine and for decades was on medicinal opium. In death, Parliament recognised his great worth. It petitioned his family to bury him in Westminster Abbey.

facing page *Am I not a Man and a Brother?* (oil on canvas). The figure of a kneeling slave with an inspiring motto was commissioned as the seal of the Society of Friends, or Quakers, in 1787. Later it was adopted as the emblem of the Anti-Slavery Society and turned into a jasper-ware cameo by Josiah Wedgwood, and soon became the most identifiable image of the Abolitionist movement. *(Wilberforce House, Hull City Museums and Art Galleries, UK; www.bridgeman.co.uk.)*

John Harrison

1693-1776

The perfectionist who, after decades of perseverance against Establishment prejudice and skulduggery, solved the greatest scientific problem of his day — how to fix longitude at sea — which was costing thousands of sailors' lives.

Yes, he was impossibly single-minded. He did not help himself. But none of Yorkshire's greatest was more shabbily treated by the elite than John Harrison, who solved the greatest scientific problem of his age and so saved countless lives.

Determining latitude at sea was a doddle. The Vikings and Columbus knew how to steer east/west or west/east by the heavens along imaginary parallels. Determining longitude was entirely another matter. Because of the spheroid shape of the Earth, these imaginary encircling lines converging at the poles mean that one degree of longitude varies in value from next to nothing at the poles to sixty-eight miles at the Equator.

Galileo and Halley, of comet fame, wrestled with the problem in vain. What they needed was a reliable clock allowing comparison with the time in the home port with noon, fixed by the sun, wherever the vessel happened to be. Every hour's difference represented fifteen degrees. Sir Isaac Newton despaired of any timepiece that was unaffected by a heaving, sea-washed deck, extremes of temperature, and variations in magnetism and barometric pressure. For want of this navigational aid, more than 2,000 seamen went to their deaths in October 1707, for example, when four British men-o'-war ran aground in the Scillies.

Seven years later the Longitude Act offered three prizes worth from £10,000 to £20,000 for methods accurately determining longitude to within one to half a degree. The enormity of the prizes and the margins of error allowed tell you how desperate they were.

Enter John Harrison. Born the eldest of five children of a carpenter at Foulby, near Pontefract, he spent his early years on Nostell Priory estate before

Oil painting of John Harrison by Thomas King from 1767. Harrison, the chronometer pioneer, is shown seated beside a table, holding the watch made to his design by John Jeffries in 1753. It took Harrison more than forty years to crack to his satisfaction the problem of determining longitude at sea. During that time he devised many other ways of improving the accuracy of timekeepers. He is pictured in front of two of his inventions: the grid-iron pendulum invented in 1726, behind him; and the H3 version of his marine chronometer, on the wall to his right. *(Science Museum Pictorial.)*

his family moved to Barrow-on-Humber, Lincolnshire. Hungry for know-ledge, he learned woodworking from his father and how to read and write and, with the help of a clergyman's books, the mechanics of motion.

He then turned to clockmaking using virtually only wood. Some are still working museum pieces. In 1730 he went to London to present his ideas to the

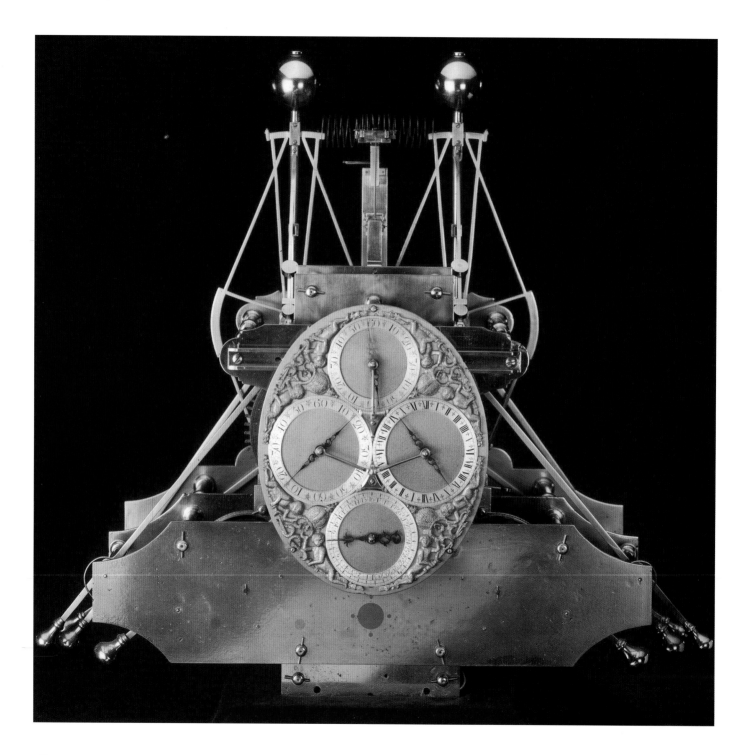

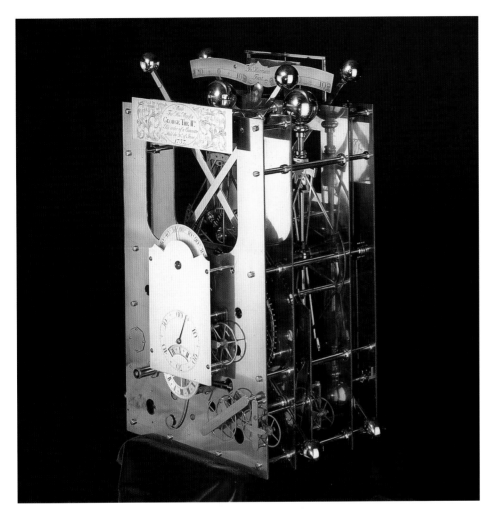

facing page Marine timekeeper H1. This is the first experimental marine timekeeper made by John Harrison in Barrow-on-Humber between 1730 and 1735 as a first step towards solving the longitude problem and winning the great £20,000 prize offered by the Government. Now known as 'H1', the timekeeper is unaffected by the motion of a ship owing to its two interconnected swinging balances. It compensates for changes in temperature and, thanks to extensive anti-friction devices, runs without any lubrication. It was the first relatively successful marine timekeeper of any kind and was the toast of London when Harrison unveiled it in 1735. (© *National Maritime Museum, London.*)

left Marine timekeeper, H2. Made between 1737 and 1739, this is a larger and more solidly built version of H1, with the additional refinement of a *remontoire* — a device to ensure that the drive to the two balances is as uniform as possible. It is probable that Harrison, who had moved to London, had some help in making parts of H2. Because he discovered a design fault with its balances, Harrison never allowed H2 to be tested at sea. (© *National Maritime Museum, London.*)

Board of Longitude administering the prizes. It had never met for want of proposed solutions, and was never likely to take seriously a mechanical solution since it was stuffed full of astronomers and mathematicians who saw it as a scientific problem. Harrison sought out Halley, the Astronomer Royal, who referred him to the premier maker of scientific instruments, 'Honest' George Graham. After a day together, Graham became Harrison's patron and Harrison went home to build his prize-winning clock.

He produced four over the years. H1, as the first is called, was hailed by the Royal Society in 1735 and performed brilliantly in a sea trial. But Harrison, the perfectionist, made the board an offer it could not refuse: a better model *this page, left* Marine timekeeper H3. Started in 1740, this third timekeeper took Harrison nearly nineteen years to build and adjust, although it was not to win him the great longitude prize: he found that he just could not persuade the two large, heavy, circular balances to keep time well enough. Nevertheless, H3 incorporates two extremely important inventions, both relevant today: the bimetallic strip (still in use worldwide in thermostats of all kinds); and the caged roller bearing, a device found in nearly all modern mechanical engineering. (© *National Maritime Museum, London.*)

this page, right The movement of H4, a longitude timekeeper designed and drawn by John Harrison, *circa* 1760-72. (*Worshipful Company of Clockmakers' Collection, UK; www.bridgeman.co.uk.*)

facing page Marine timekeeper H4. This is Harrison's prize-winning longitude watch, completed in 1759. Harrison had been working on improving watches as a sideline to his development of the much larger H3. In 1753 a pocket watch was made to Harrison's design by watchmaker John Jefferys. This went so well that Harrison began to realise that it pointed to the longitude solution — not in H3 but in smaller watches. Work began on H4 in 1755 and, with its very stable high-frequency balance, it proved the successful design. It is shown here at almost actual size. (© *National Maritime Museum, London.*)

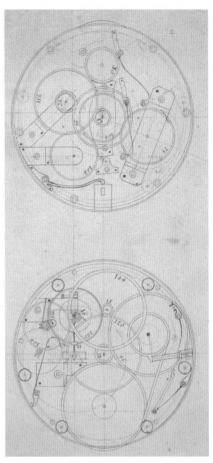

for £500 seed money. H2 emerged in 1741 but still wasn't good enough for Harrison, even though it passed rigorous tests. At the age of forty-eight he disappeared into his workshop for nearly twenty years before producing a more compact H3 with 753 separate parts. Then a clockmaker gave him a pocket watch for his personal use. This inspired him to produce in 1759 his 'beautiful and curious' H4 with a diameter of five inches and weighing three pounds.

This was the clock that won him the award — and Captain Cook's admiration — but only after fourteen years' evaluation, procrastination, chopping and changing the rules, and downright skulduggery by the astronomy establishment who would not give second best to a self-taught Yorkshireman. In the end George III thought Harrison and his gifted son had been 'cruelly treated' and swore to see them 'righted'.

King Edwin

c 585-633

No, the greatest Yorkshire monarch was not that 'noble son of York', Richard III. He was born at Fotheringay Castle in Northamptonshire. But we do have a choice. It is between a saint and a sinner: Edwin, King of Deira; and Henry I, the youngest son of William the Conqueror. I have chosen the saint.

Edwin was canonised after his conversion of Yorkshire — and effectively the North of England — to Christianity in AD 627. He established a bishopric at York, and became recognised as a Christian warrior and martyr. The church dedicated shrines to him in York and Whitby, where his remains were eventually interred.

Henry was our most prolific monarch. He beat James II by two children, but only four of his twenty-nine offspring were legitimate. He is also suspected of masterminding the killing of his brother, William Rufus (William II), in the New Forest while another brother, Robert, duke of Normandy, was away at the Crusades so that he could seize the throne — as he did, with unseemly haste. Yet he was a capable king who presided over the height of Norman might. He was also the first Norman king to be able to read and write because, as Henry Beauclerc ('fine scholar'), he had been intended for Holy Orders.

Henry was a Yorkshireman by accident — born at Selby while his father was in York putting down an early revolt. Edwin, son of Aelle, who established an Angle kingdom in Deira — the early Yorkshire — in AD 569, was, however, a true Yorkshire lad who came into this world around 585, probably at Goodmanham near Market Weighton.

Edwin was not born to rule any more than Henry was, and for years it

In 1878, the celebrated Pre-Raphaelite artist Ford Madox Brown was commissioned to paint wall murals for the newly built Manchester Town Hall. The twelve murals — including *The Baptism of Edwin, King of Northumbria and Deira*, shown opposite — eventually took Madox Brown fifteen years to complete. *(Manchester City Council.)*

seemed he never would. His elder brother, Athelric, a pitiable sort, lost his throne and life in 604 to Athelfrith of Bernicia, the neighbouring kingdom to the north. Athelfrith would have had Edwin's life, too, pursuing him for more than ten years through Gwynedd and Powys in North Wales, Mercia and East Anglia. He tried to bribe East Anglia's Redwald to murder him. Instead, Redwald rode against Athelfrith and cut him down at the Battle of the River Idle, near Bawtry (616).

Edwin recovered Deira and, embarking on total conquest, established the English in the North. By AD 625 he dominated the North of England.

Two years later he converted to Christianity under the influence of his second wife Athelburh, Christian daughter of the king of Kent, and Paulinus, an Italian missionary whom he made the first bishop of York. His conversion came after a narrow escape from assassination by a West Saxon on the day his wife gave birth to a daughter. But he apparently agreed only on condition that Paulinus' God granted him victory over the West Saxons.

Six years of peace and prosperity followed until Caedwalla had revenge in 633 when he slew Edwin and his two sons at the Battle of Hatfield Chase, near Doncaster. Instead of claiming Northumbria, Caedwalla devastated it, but it rose again from the ashes and Edwin's bishopric ensured that Christianity prevailed.

Henry's life fell apart when his two legitimate sons were drowned. He left no male heir and in desperation made his barons swear reluctant fealty to his daughter, Matilda. He met his death on the warpath in Normandy from ptomaine food poisoning after gorging himself on his weakness — lampreys. Edwin bequeathed Christianity; Henry, civil war.

Alcuin

c 732-804

Charlemagne's cultural dynamo, the foremost scholar in the revival of learning who paved the way for Europe's intellectual renaissance.

Just over a century after King Edwin had converted Yorkshire to Christianity, a Northumbrian noblewoman gave birth to a son in or near York. Alhwin, or Alcuin as he is known, became the major agent in the revival of learning in Charlemagne's Holy Roman Empire.

The achievements of this much-loved scholar, teacher, theologian and liturgist were prodigious, whether as a headmaster in York, as Charlemagne's cultural adviser in Aachen or in 'retirement' as abbot of Tours in France. He had a formative influence in the development of Roman Catholicism, notably by revising the liturgy of the Frankish Church, introducing the Irish Northumbrian custom of singing the creed, arranging votive masses for particular days of the week in an order still followed, and re-editing the Latin Vulgate. He is even credited with making possible the European intellectual renaissance three centuries later.

Alcuin entered Archbishop Egbert's cathedral school in York at a tender age. His aptitude was cultivated by both Egbert and his master Aelbert and, when Aelbert succeeded Egbert to the archbishopric, Alcuin took over the school.

He became the schoolmaster of the age. His humility and sanctity, and his enthusiasm for learning and teaching, inspired many of the young men of talent whom he drew to York from all over the Christian world to become religious leaders. He toured Europe, collecting and copying books, and built up a precious library in York, including his poem *On the Saints of the Church of York*, a valuable description of the city's academic life.

'Christ in Majesty with the Symbols of the Evangelists', illustration on vellum from The Bible of Alcuin completed in AD 801. The Alcuin Bible is a perfect example of Carolingian book illustration, which combined the Byzantine and Celtic artistic styles, complemented by lavish use of gold leaf decoration. *(British Museum, London, UK; www.bridgeman.co.uk.)*

After fifty years in York, he met Charlemagne in Italy in AD 781 while returning to England from Rome, and was persuaded to take over the emperor's palace school. Charlemagne himself, his queen, three sons and two daughters became pupils. Alcuin organised studies on modern lines with classes and specialist teachers for each subject. His school became the European centre of knowledge and culture, and the inspiration for an imperial decree establishing primary schools in every town and village of the empire. He also developed the Carolingian miniscule, a clear script that is the ancestor of modern Roman typefaces.

In AD 796 the emperor, who perhaps too often sent Alcuin on missions abroad, allowed him to retire from the world as abbot of St Martin's at Tours. There he set up a model monastic school, and again collected books and students. He died in office around the age of seventy, having made the rich intellectual inheritance of Bede at Jarrow and Anglo-Saxon scholarship the property of civilised Europe.

Yet for all his towering achievements, Alcuin may never have advanced beyond a deacon of the Church. He acquired a reputation for holiness, but was never admitted to the canon of saints. He perhaps feared Charlemagne as much as he loved him. His writings are judged to show no originality and his poetry to be mostly mediocre. But then he was a teacher rather than a thinker; a gatherer, conserver and distributor rather than an originator of knowledge. His motto was: 'Learn in order to teach'. He was just what the eighth century needed — a collector and preserver of knowledge inherited from a violent past. Alcuin: Yorkshire's — and Europe's — first educator.

facing page Emperor Charlemagne Surrounded by his Principal Officers, Receiving Alcuin (c 735-804) who is Presenting some Manuscripts made by his Monks (oil on canvas) by Jean Victor Schnetz. (Louvre, Paris, France/www.bridgeman.co.uk.)

John Wycliffe

c 1330-84

'The flower of Oxford' whose battle against church abuses paved the way for the Protestant Reformation and the promoter of the first complete translation of the Bible into English.

If Alcuin fathered the intellectual renaissance of Europe, John Wycliffe surely sired the Reformation. He was born at Hipswell, near Richmond, into a wealthy family and a land in the grip of a debauched, predatory Church. He went to Oxford around the age of thirteen to study the scriptures and became the 'flower of Oxford' — a devout polymath, if ever there was one, his inquiring mind ranging over optics, chemical analysis, economics, geometry, mathematics and even the physiology of sleep.

But he was preoccupied with the word of God that to him was a beacon in a world of spiritual darkness. He was deeply affected by the 'judgement' of the Black Death that carried away nearly half the population from 1348. Yet it was not until he resigned as master of Balliol in 1361 for a succession of church livings that this spare, frail and simple man came out of his shell to demonstrate a formidable, driven courage of conviction.

His belief in the doctrine that Christ is man's only overlord made him a forthright champion of the people against Church abuses. He argued that man exercised 'dominion' from God and that the righteous alone could properly have dominion. As the Church was in sin, it should give up its possessions and return to poverty.

He first railed against mendicant friars — beggars diverting alms from the needy to the enrichment of their monasteries. Then, as a chaplain to the king, he was sent to Bruges in 1365 to negotiate with Rome on papal taxes and appointments to church posts. Pope Urban V sought to re-assert the Church's authority over England and demanded back payment of its annual tribute

By definition, we do not know what so many Yorkshire Greats looked like, so far back in history do we go. But what is interesting about John Wycliffe is how similar 'portraits' of him look. This is one fictitious portrait called John Wycliffe by Conrad Meyer. *(Courtesy National Portrait Gallery, London.)*

John Wycliffe reading his translation of
the Bible to John of Gaunt (oil on
canvas, 1847-8) by Ford Madox Brown.
(Bradford Art Galleries and Museums/
www.bridgeman.co.uk.)

that had lapsed thirty years earlier. King and parliament rejected the demand,
believing, among other things, that Rome's money financed enemy armies.

Wycliffe was clear: 'There cannot be two temporal sovereigns in one
country. Either Edward is king or Urban is king. We accept Edward of
England and refuse Urban of Rome.' He returned from Bruges after two
years, convinced that the Pope was the anti-Christ. He campaigned, little by
little but with passion and conviction, against Church practices and doctrine.

One of the most intriguing facts about John Wycliffe is that he was allowed to die in his bed. He was a most uncomfortable Yorkshireman — and nobody's poodle. Not surprisingly we have a picture of him preaching to a group of alarmed Franciscans from his bed, circa 1380. *(Hulton Archive/ Getty Images.)*

He survived five papal bulls and show trials for heresy because he had the powerful support, no doubt for their own ends, of John of Gaunt and Lord Percy, Earl Marshal of England.

Then he went too far. His systematic attack on the Church's beliefs included transubstantiation — that the bread and wine of the Eucharist are changed into the body and blood of Christ. His ingenuousness — he was no calculating priest-politician — eventually cost him even Oxford's support.

He retired in 1381 to his Lutterworth living to superintend the completion of the translation of the Bible into English for the benefit of the people and to see his works condemned in Synod, and to die of yet another stroke. He left behind his disciples, the Lollards, ascetic, peripatetic priests who preached the word of God and Wycliffe's views to a receptive populace. They were, of course, persecuted for it. The wonder is that Wycliffe was allowed to die in his bed.

To this day he excites a variety of emotions. He may have been politically naïve and used by the powerful, but he is generally recognised as having been devout and sincere, and not least a powerfully influential forerunner of the Reformation.

William Bradford

1590-1657

The greatest Pilgrim Father of them all, who governed the Plymouth Harbor colony in New England for most of its first thirty-seven years, establishing a tradition of democratic self-government in America.

Of the 102 passengers crammed into the *Mayflower*, William Bradford was the greatest Pilgrim Father of them all. He was a key organiser of 'the weighty voyage', governor of the fledgling colony for all bar five of its first thirty-seven years until his death and originator of that unique American celebration, Thanksgiving. He also wrote the only complete history of the colony by a *Mayflower* passenger, *Of Plymouth Plantation 1620-47*.

If ever there was a survivor, it was Bradford. Born just in Yorkshire in the farming community of Austerfield, near Bawtry, he was orphaned of parents and grandparents by the age of seven and brought up with an older sister by an uncle. A sickly child, he had by the age of twelve taken to reading the Bible, and become drawn to the Separatist Church on the left of the Puritan movement by their fellowship and lack of ritual. By the time he was eigthteen he was potentially a wanted man because the Church of England was trying to snuff out these rival sects. When James I announced his intention to 'harry them from the land', they sought refuge in Holland.

For twelve years Bradford and his fellow exiles eked out a living as textile workers, first in Amsterdam, where he married, and then in Leiden. Under pressure from King James, the Dutch in turn began to harass them. They resolved to seek religious freedom 'some place about Hudson's river'. Bradford was at the heart of the planning and preparatory work, and had to make the awful choice temporarily to leave behind his four-year-old son because not everyone could go.

After a sixty-six day storm-tossed and near-mutinous voyage, with leaking upper decks and a cracked main beam, they made landfall to the north in New

A one-sixtieth scale model of the *Mayflower*. In 1620, fleeing religious persecution, 102 Puritans organised by William Bradford and led by John Carver set sail from Plymouth, seeking to establish a colony in the New World. Sixty-six days later, blown off their intended course for Virginia, they came ashore on Cape Cod, and established a settlement which they named New Plymouth. The ship in which the Pilgrim Fathers sailed was an ordinary small merchant ship of the period. The decoration has been copied from the geometric patterns shown in the manuscript *Fragments of Ancient English Shipwrightry* by Matthew Baker, with the addition of a conventional 'mayflower' on the stern. The rig of a small merchant ship of this period was likely to have been the ordinary three-masted arrangement. *(Science Museum, London.)*

England, utterly exhausted. And there, anchored off Cape Cod, before they had even found Plymouth Harbor in which to settle, Bradford's wife, Dorothy, fell overboard and was drowned. Within five months half the remaining Pilgrims, including the first elected governor, succumbed to the starving winter. Bradford was ill, too, but recovered to take over the colony's leadership. He was re-elected thirty times and had only five year-long respites from responsibility until his death.

He forged a relationship with the Wampanoag Indians, and by the autumn of 1621 the surviving Pilgrims had recovered their health, harvested the Indian corn and 'fitted their houses against the winter'. Bradford called for a

Jolyon Rollins portrays Governor William Bradford in his house at Plimoth Plantation, a recreation of the original Plymouth Colony as it would have appeared in 1627, six years after the first Thanksgiving festival. *(Photo by Michael Springer/Getty Images.)*

celebration — the very first Thanksgiving. He married a widow who provided a home for the son he had left behind as well as her own two children and the three she had with him. He served as a judge and negotiator with the Dutch in New York and the new Massachusetts Bay colony, and was responsible for maintaining friendly relations with the native people. While he called himself a Congregationalist, he discouraged sectarian labels and welcomed all

Separatist groups to the colony. Sadly, he lived to be distressed by the loss of Plymouth's original fellowship as settlers moved out in search of land.

Bradford's will to survive — his true Yorkshire grit — his moral and physical stamina, his gift for managing men's affairs, and his faith and vision were the rock on which the New World was built. Not the least of his achievements was to set the pattern for the political development of America, land of the free.

The First Thanksgiving (oil on canvas) by Jean Leon Jerome Ferris (1863-1930). *(Private Collection, USA.)*

John Smeaton

1724-92

*The founder of civil engineering
as a profession who built the
Eddystone lighthouse and was
responsible for a breathtaking
array of projects that facilitated
the Industrial Revolution.*

You name it, he built it. Canals, harbours, bridges, docks, wind, water and
steam mills, pumping engines and, of course, lighthouses. They are part of
our national heritage along with virtually all his high-quality and detailed
drawings preserved in the Library of the Royal Society, to which he was
elected at twenty-eight. Mind you, none of this would have happened if his
father had had his way. Smeaton senior wanted his serious-minded elder son,
John, to be a lawyer like himself.

John had other ideas. In his six years at Leeds Grammar School he devoted
himself to mechanics in his workshop at his comfortable home at Austhorpe
Lodge, Whitkirk. His interest was reinforced after meeting a gifted York
clock- and instrument-maker. He was dispatched to London at eighteen for a
legal education, but he stuck it for only two years. By then he had met another
lad from Leeds, Benjamin Wilson, who was to abandon law for painting and
experiments with electricity. Smeaton returned home to build mathematical
instruments and apparatus for Wilson's experiments, and to study astronomy.

In 1748 his parents capitulated to the inevitable. He was allowed to set himself up in business as an instrument maker in London, where he came to rank
with the greatest of the day. He produced an improved vacuum pump, helped
develop the Royal Navy's standard compass, anticipated the production of the
ship's log, and built telescopes and a precision lathe.

He also took his first step towards engineering, experimenting with water
and wind power. By 1753 the instrument maker had decided 'engineery' would
be his career His guiding principle was: 'One thing done well recommends

Portrait of John Smeaton (oil on canvas, 1779) by George Romney — with the inevitable lighthouse in the background. *(By courtesy of the National Portrait Gallery, London.)*

another'. It served him admirably. He invented a new form of pulley tackle, designed a cofferdam for the repair of Westminster Bridge, built wind and water mills, and designed the draining of Dumfriesshire peatland. In 1765 he went to study canals, harbours and mills in the Low Countries. It was five weeks well spent. Lord Macclesfield, president of the Royal Society, recommended him to rebuild Eddystone Lighthouse, successively destroyed by storm and fire, just as he was about to marry a York girl.

He devoted four years (1756-9) to building Eddystone on a gale-swept crag off Plymouth, using dovetailed blocks of Cornish granite to withstand the waves. This construction became standard practice. When he could not work on the lighthouse in winter, he developed his engineering business with a host of navigation schemes. He returned to live in the family home at Austhorpe, where he built a new workshop and began a new phase in his life as a professional civil engineer. It involved the transition from wind and water power to steam.

His best-known works are the Calder and Hebble Navigation from Wakefield to Sowerby Bridge, the Forth and Clyde Canal linking the North Sea with the Atlantic, Ramsgate Harbour, bridges in Perth, Banff and Coldstream, and the docks at Kronstadt, Russia. He was involved in at least sixty-five mill and other mechanical projects, thirteen steam engines and thirty-six civil engineering projects including, in Yorkshire, Potteric Carr, Adlingfleet and Hatfield Chase, Ure Navigation and Ripon Canal, Spurn Lighthouse, Aire and Calder Navigation, and Hull North Bridge. He was a founder member of the Society of Civil Engineers, later called the Smeatonian Society. He died from a stroke in his garden. His daughter summed up his life as 'active as useful, amiable as revered'.

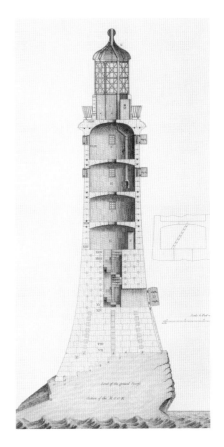

above Smeaton's Eddystone Lighthouse engraved by Edward Rooker in 1763. *(Private Collection, the Stapleton Collection/www.bridgeman.co.uk.)*

facing page *A Man of War passing the Eddystone Lighthouse* (oil on canvas, c 1773) by Francis Holman. *(Fitzwilliam Museum, University of Cambridge, UK/www.bridgeman.co.uk.)*

William Bateson

1861-1926

The forthright founder of the science of genetics — and originator of the term — who provided the evidence basic to the modern understanding of heredity.

The founder of the science of genetics — and originator of the term — may be little more of a Yorkshireman than Henry I who happened to be born in the county. Yet William Bateson exhibited the awkward, unbending traits of a true Yorkshireman in his academic arguments — and he was born in Whitby. He is not a household name there, but since his sister Mary, an eminent Cambridge historian, was born in Robin Hood's Bay, the family has more than a passing association with the North Yorkshire coast.

Much more is known about Bateson's genes. He was the second of six children of the reformist Master of St John's College, Cambridge — William Henry Bateson. All the children were academically inclined, and inherited their parents' independence of mind and headstrong, disputatious nature.

At Rugby, William did not get much encouragement for his interest in natural history, which had been fired by Darwin's new theories, and came out with an indifferent academic record. But he excelled in zoology at St John's, Cambridge, and made his name with two years' postgraduate study of embryology in America of the obscure 'worm' called *balanoglossus*. This led him to conclude that primitive echinoderms evolved into vertebrates — a view now widely accepted. His work earned him a fellowship at St John's.

After two years studying the fauna of salt lakes in Europe, Central Asia and Egypt, he returned to Cambridge to immerse himself for seven years in the central problems of the Darwinian theory — the mechanism of heredity and the nature of variations. He painstakingly accumulated data on variations in species, and by 1894 this ardent Darwinian had developed a theory that

One of the candidates for the Yorkshire Greats was Sir William Rothenstein (1872-1945), the Bradford-born artist. He became professor of fine art at Sheffield University, and principal of the Royal College of Art. We pay tribute to him in this book with this pencil drawing of the zoologist and geneticist William Bateson from 1917. *(By courtesy of the National Portrait Gallery, London.)*

Such was William Bateson's passion for genetics that he gave up a new chair in the subject at Cambridge University within two years for the much better funded directorship of the John Innes Institute, then in Merton, Surrey. Here we see Bateson in the institute gardens. *(Archive Collection, John Innes Centre.)*

implied the evolutionary process was radically different — and riddled with discontinuities — from the gradual incrementalism predicted by Darwin. He won few converts with his forcefully argued case, but he self-confidently turned to experiment, recognising that discontinuities could only be understood if something was known about the inheritance of traits.

Then in 1900 he discovered an article 'Experiments with Plant Hybrids', written thirty-four years earlier by an Austrian monk, Gregor Mendel, which explained perfectly his breeding results. He translated Mendel's paper into English and became his champion in England. By experiment he extended Mendel's principles from plants to animals — specifically, poultry — and discovered a phenomenon called linkage, apparently counter to Mendel, which showed that certain features were consistently inherited together. This is now known to be the result of genes closely located on the same chromosome.

Bateson, misinterpreting the results of his research, would have none of this chromosome theory and indulged in splendidly intemperate academic rows with the Galtonian chromosome theorists. He still excites scientists' angst, demonstrating that his Yorkshire genes were in proper working order to the end.

He was not backwards in coming forwards either. Applying for a university chair in the study of heredity and variation, he suggested that a new word was badly needed for the subject 'and if it were desirable to coin one, genetics might do'. It did, though he had to wait three years before he was awarded the new chair in genetics at Cambridge. Within two years he was off to the better-endowed directorship of the John Innes Institute (now known as the John Innes Centre), then in Merton, Surrey, and now in Norwich. Over the rest of his life, scarred by the tragic deaths of two of his gifted sons, he transformed the institute into a centre for genetic research.

Bateson in the lab at the John Innes Institute. (*Archive Collection, John Innes Centre.*)

Joseph Bramah

1748-1814

The ploughboy who, lamed for life, turned inventor and became the father of the machine-tool industry, the mainspring of the Industrial Revolution.

What, I wonder, would have become of Joseph Bramah had he not broken his ankle as a sixteen-year-old working on his father's farm at Stainborough, near Barnsley, and lamed himself for life? Would he have blossomed as a craftsman and prolific inventor, and eventually become renowned as the father of the British machine-tool industry, the basis for the vast expansion of British industry in the nineteenth century? It is impossible to say, but it seems unlikely.

A broken ankle in the eighteenth century was a serious matter, but it was the making of the farmer's son. With no more than a basic education, he had shown an aptitude for building musical instruments with rudimentary tools before the accident rendered him useless on the farm. He then turned to woodwork, and the problem of an unproductive mouth to feed — he was the eldest of five children — was solved when he was apprenticed to the village carpenter. No sooner had he finished his apprenticeship than he did a Dick Whittington and, disabled though he was, walked to London to seek fame and fortune.

After working as a cabinetmaker, he set himself up in business and turned inventor. His first invention, patented in 1778, was an improved version of the modern water-closet he had been installing as part of his business. He then rose to the challenge of the lock. Man had been using locks of a sort since the Ancient Egyptians, but they remained notoriously pickable. In 1784 Bramah patented his secure lock. In 1801 he put one made by his partner Henry Maudslay in his shop window and offered the handsome reward of £200 to the first person who unpicked it. It was not until fifty years later, long

left Oil painting of Joseph Bramah (1749-1814). Bramah made numerous inventions, including a beer machine used at the bar of public houses, a safety lock which he manufactured in partnership with Henry Maudslay (1771-1831), and an ingenious machine for printing banknotes. Bramah invented a hydraulic press for shaping pieces of iron and steel, considered one of the great instruments of the Industrial Revolution. *(Science Museum Pictorial.)*

facing page Challenge board for the Bramah padlock from 1801. The lock was placed in the window of Bramah and Co's shop with a board offering a reward. The lock stayed in the window un-picked for fifty years until 1851 when it was opened by A C Hobbs, an American locksmith, who came to London for the Great Exhibition and took on the challenge. He took sixteen days to open the lock and receive his reward. Chubb now own Hobbs' world-famous firm. *(Science Museum.)*

Five lock templates dating from *circa* 1780 used for the drilling of Bramah locks. Joseph Bramah made numerous inventions, including a safety lock which he manufactured in partnership with Henry Maudslay. *(Science Museum.)*

after Bramah's death, that a skilled American locksmith claimed his reward — after working at it for fifty-one hours over sixteen days, using a variety of instruments.

The action of the lock depended on the precision of the parts, and mass production of a quality product required machine tools. He joined forces with another gifted lad, an eighteen-year-old blacksmith, Henry Maudslay, then at the Woolwich Arsenal. He was an engineering genius. Together Bramah and Maudslay invented over thirty years a host of machines of fundamental importance to the Industrial Revolution. Bramah's sons joined the family business, and their father's signature is still its twenty-first century trademark.

If there was a mechanical problem, Bramah, it seemed, would crack it. At one stage he held more than twenty patents. In 1795 he invented the hydraulic

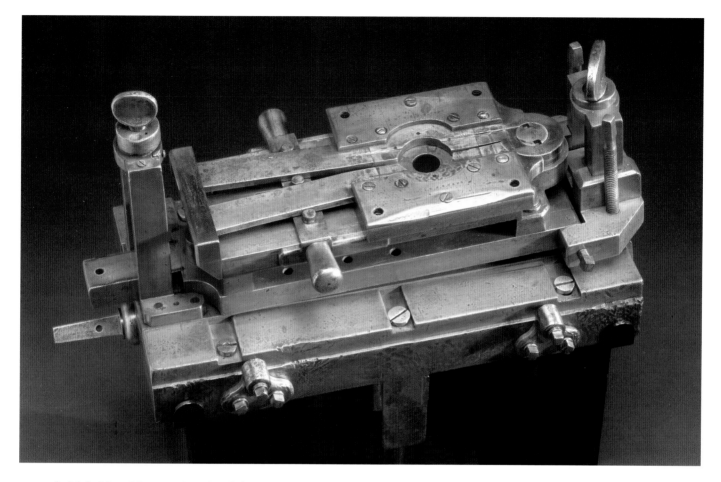

press (which Maudslay made reliable) and two years later the beer pump that eventually made 'jug runners' — staff bringing beer up from the cellar to the tables — redundant. His other inventions were a fire engine, a quill sharpener and a machine for making quill pens, wood and metal planes and, at the behest of the Bank of England — and in a mere matter of a month — a machine for accurately numbering banknotes.

His last was a machine for applying cement to timber to prevent dry rot. Bramah died suddenly at the age of sixty-six in 1814 after catching a cold that turned to pneumonia in Holt Forest, Hampshire, superintending one of his hydraulic machines tearing up 300 trees by the roots. His machines were not his only legacy to the nation. He also provided a supply of top-class mechanics to drive forward the Industrial Revolution.

Bramah's special vice of 1790, made to be used attached to a lathe. (*Science Museum.*)

Lieut-Gen Augustus Henry Lane-Fox Pitt-Rivers

1827-1900

The father of British archaeology and most certainly the progenitor of modern scientific archaeology.

A crusty perfectionist lies behind all those fascinating television programmes about digging up our ancestors. He is called the father of British archaeology, though his greater claim to fame is the father of modern scientific archaeology. His name is the biggest mouthful in this book of Yorkshire Greats.

He was born Augustus Henry Lane-Fox into a prominent Yorkshire family at Hope Hall, Bramham. He adopted the name Pitt-Rivers after his great-uncle, who in 1880 bequeathed him the 29,000-acre Cranborne Chase estate on the Dorset-Wiltshire border. It was on that estate that he made archaeology a systematic, painstaking, scientific study of the past. Few, if any, explored the history lying in our land as meticulously as he did.

Pitt-Rivers, as he is known with or without the hyphen, went to Sandhurst, was mentioned in dispatches in the Crimea and for most of his thirty-seven-year army career in the Grenadier Guards was a staff officer. But he wasn't just a professional soldier. He was fascinated by man's development, and his research from 1851 on the replacement of muskets with rifles led to the study of the development of firearms. That, in turn, led to an interest in artefacts and their arrangement in 'a chronological, developmental sequence'.

His approach coincided with or was inspired by Darwin's theory of evolution, and he sought to explore man's material cultural development in a similar 'genetic' way. He named the process 'typology' and applied it to weaponry, tools and implements, and dress and ornaments. He believed typology 'forms a tree of progress and distinguishes the leading shoots from the inner branches' and was the 'key to the whole of human culture'.

This somewhat Napoleonic studio portrait of General Pitt-Rivers has him looking into the far distance. This is entirely appropriate, for if any Yorkshireman made it his calling to look deep into the past and make sense of it, it was Augustus Pitt-Rivers. *(Pitt Rivers Museum, University of Oxford.)*

At thirty-seven feet high, the totem pole at the Pitt Rivers Museum is the largest object on display. The totem pole, carved from red cedar, is from a Haida community in British Columbia, Canada. The pole came to the Pitt Rivers Museum in 1901. It was bought for $36, and shipped by rail and steamer. To make transporting the pole easier, it was cut in two and the raven's beak removed. The pole was originally raised at a 'potlatch', a ceremony at which a person is given traditional family rights. The pole is carved with crest figures that relate to family lineages, status and rights, just as noble European families had crests depicting their status. The carvings remind viewers of the stories of how ancestral beings bestowed certain rights and property on a family. The figures depicted on this pole are, from the top: three seated figures or watchmen; bear eating a frog with a bear cub between its legs; bear holding a human with two bear cubs at its feet; and a raven with a human between its wings. *(B.67.269.9/Pitt Rivers Museum, University of Oxford.)*

He is known to have carried out some limited excavations during his service in Ireland (1862-6). But his opportunity for serious exploration came with his inheritance. He retired from the army in 1882, and the following year embarked on seventeen seasons of excavation of prehistoric, Roman and Saxon sites on Cranborne Chase, unearthing villages, camps, cemeteries, and barrows or burial mounds.

Unlike so many others, he was not looking for treasure but for knowledge. He saw archaeology as a means of producing 'the long timescale necessary to establish an evolutionary sequence' by total excavation, stratigraphic observation and accurate recording. This meant examining the ordinary things of life left by our ancestors, including their rubbish.

His systematic approach and attention to detail made him a hard taskmaster. He required his assistants, employed on a stipend, to be skilled surveyors and draftsmen in three dimensions. They dug and recorded a site layer by layer. He certainly produced the evidence. In one excavated village in which an archaeologist had reported finding nothing, his methods uncovered ninety-seven pits and fifteen skeletons. He amassed some of the most highly regarded archaeological data and sumptuously published it in one of the classics of archaeology, *Excavations in Cranborne Chase*.

Pitt-Rivers became the country's first inspector of ancient monuments after his future son-in-law had secured the passage of the Ancient Monuments Act of 1882. He was also an educationist. He believed that the facts of evolution could be taught by museums, and made a vast number of artefacts available to the public through the Farnham and Bethnal Green Museums, and the one which bears his name in Oxford. The Salisbury and South Wiltshire Museum devotes a gallery to his work and the material he excavated. He was no ordinary soldier — or general.

Two men on the Andaman Islands, India, *circa* 1875. One holds a bow, the other is wearing a belt *boda*, a shell-decorated cincture, and head, neck, arm and leg ornaments decorated with vegetable fibre and shells; behind them is a *pu-kuta-yemnga* sounding board. This photograph was one of thousands donated by Pitt-Rivers in 1884 to found the museum named after him. *(1998.230.18/Pitt Rivers Museum, University of Oxford.)*

Joseph Priestley

1733-1804

The brilliant parson, political theorist, educator and scientist who discovered oxygen and was forced to seek civil and religious liberty in America.

Joseph Priestley, from Birstall, near Leeds, was a phenomenon in a century dazzled by gifted Yorkshiremen. There was no end to his talents, even if he was largely self-taught. Nor were there limits to his capacity for making enemies, which explains why he died in Pennsylvania.

This polymath was the eldest of a successful cloth-dresser's six children. He

left A portrait of Joseph Priestley circa 1797 by James Sharples. *(By courtesy of the National Portrait Gallery, London.)*

facing page left The Rev Austin Fitzpatrick, former minister of Mill Hill Chapel, lays a spray of white roses at the base of Priestley's statue in City Square, Leeds, on the 200th anniversary of Priestley's death in February 2004. *(Photo by Kate Taylor.)*

facing page right Fieldhead, Birstall, where Joseph Priestley was born in March 1733. *(Painting by Stephen Barlow.)*

A reconstruction painting of the building now known as the Old Hall, Heckmondwike, in 1745. Priestley lived there as a child with his aunt Sarah and uncle John Keighley. *(Painting by Stephen Barlow.)*

All Saints Church, the vicarage, the Golden Fleece inn and Batley Free Grammar School in 1745 — the same year that Priestley started as a pupil there, and where he learned Greek, Latin and an early form of shorthand. *(Painting by Stephen Barlow.)*

had a sickly childhood, but that helped rather than hindered his pursuit of knowledge. He just studied. His Calvinist parents wanted him to enter the Dissenting ministry, and to that end he studied 'Hebrew, Chaldee, Syriac and a little Arabic' with the help of a Nonconformist parson. He continued his studies at a new Dissenting academy at Daventry, Northants, established for Nonconformists, where he went far beyond the requirements of the curriculum in his study of history, philosophy and science.

For all his devotion, his first ministry at Needham Market, Suffolk, in 1755 was not a success. He frightened his orthodox congregation with his views as he tried to sort out his religious convictions — a process that ended with his embracing Unitarianism, denying the Trinity. He found a more sympathetic flock in Nantwich, Cheshire, where his success with a school he opened led to

An engraving of the original Mill Hill Chapel, Leeds, before rebuilding. The first chapel was constructed in 1674. The rebuilt chapel which stands today in City Square was designed by Bowman & Crowther and opened in December 1848. Priestley became minister at the original chapel pictured here in 1767, receiving a stipend of 100 guineas and living in the minister's house north of the chapel. *(Courtesy Leeds Library & Information Services.)*

his engagement as tutor in language and literature at Warrington Academy. This was an inspired appointment at a time when universities and professions were closed to Dissenters. He prepared students for careers in industry and commerce with his own courses and textbooks, and made the academy the most distinguished of its kind in England. He was ordained in 1762 when he married.

In the mid-1760s he turned increasingly to study science. His meeting with Benjamin Franklin in London led him to experiment with electricity and produce within two years an original work summarising existing knowledge of the subject. His move to Mill Hill Chapel in Leeds in 1767 gave him more time for writing and experiment, this time into gases, stimulated by living next door to a brewery. Over the years he discovered ten gases, including laughing gas, ammonia, sulphur dioxide, carbon monoxide and in 1774 oxygen, which he called 'dephlogisticated air'. It was left to Lavoisier to name it oxygen. He also discovered how to carbonate water and won the Royal Society's Copley Medal for all his work.

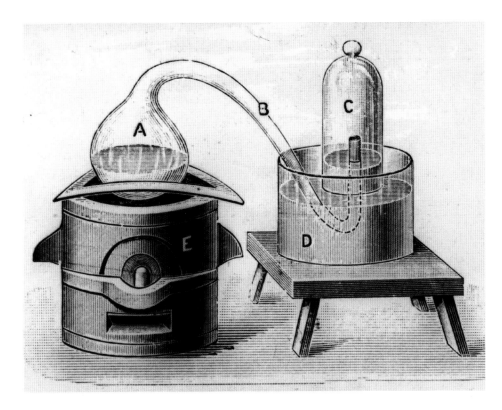

He then worked for seven years as a tutor to the Earl of Shelburne's family in Wiltshire, with freedom to write and preach as he wished. Increasing opposition to his religious views caused him to turn down an invitation to join Captain Cook's second voyage. Then in 1779 he went as a minister to Birmingham where, in its Lunar Society, dedicated to applied science, he debated with the likes of Smeaton, Wedgwood, Watt and Erasmus Darwin, Charles' naturalist grandfather. These were his happiest and busiest years, but his promotion of civil and religious liberty, and his support for the principles of the French Revolution, roused the mob.

On the second anniversary of the fall of the Bastille in 1791, his house, library and laboratory were destroyed. He fled to London and then, when war was declared with France, followed his three sons to America in 1793. He was welcomed by Jefferson and John Adams, but his scientific if not his religious work suffered from being cut off from his friends in England. He died a victim of the intolerance he had so long fought. He is honoured with statues in City Square, Leeds, and Birstall Market.

facing page top   The Leeds Library, which Priestley was instrumental in founding in 1768, and which thrives to this day. *(Photo by Kate Taylor.)*

facing page bottom   The interior of Mill Hill Chapel, Leeds, in Priestley's time. *(Courtesy Rev Paul Travis.)*

above left   The laboratory apparatus used by Joseph Priestley circa 1774 to isolate 'dephlogisticated air' or oxygen by heating red oxide of mercury and collecting the gas: A, retort containing material to be heated; B, neck of the retort; C, inverted bell-jar evacuated of air; D, bath of mercury; E, stove. *(Photo by Hulton Archive/Getty Images.)*

above right   The memorial tablet to Joseph Priestley in Birmingham's New Meeting Unitarian Chapel. *(Photo by Kate Taylor.)*

Henry Briggs

1561-1630

The mathematician who brought logarithms to the relief of his colleagues, astronomers and other scientists, and whose tables remained in general use for more than 200 years.

He did not actually invent logarithms as a tool. That distinction lies with the Scottish genius, John Napier. But Henry Briggs, one of Halifax's most distinguished sons, was responsible for securing their acceptance and widespread use in Europe. His invention of common, or Briggsian, logarithms greatly eased the burden of his fellow mathematicians, astronomers and other scientists in making their hitherto laborious calculations. His contribution to scientific development is almost literally incalculable.

Briggs' parents were 'humble of class and rather slender of means' and brought him into this world at Daisy Bank in the Pennine hamlet of Warley, overlooking my native upper Calder Valley which has, incidentally, produced three Nobel prize-winning scientists. He was educated locally, and became highly proficient in Latin and Greek. By some means unknown, he was admitted as a scholar to St John's College, Cambridge, in 1577. Eleven years later he became a Fellow there, and his wide range of talents brought him in 1592 appointments as both medical and mathematics lecturer. In 1596 he became the first professor of geometry at Gresham College, London, the birthplace of the Royal Society, and held that post for twenty-three years.

Primarily a mathematician, Briggs became interested in astronomy and the study of eclipses. This required many laborious calculations, so he produced and published two tables to aid calculation before he read about Napier's logarithms. He then set about improving Lord Napier's system by rebasing it, and travelled the four days by coach to Edinburgh to discuss it with the lord of Merchiston Castle. He discovered that Napier had had the same idea but felt

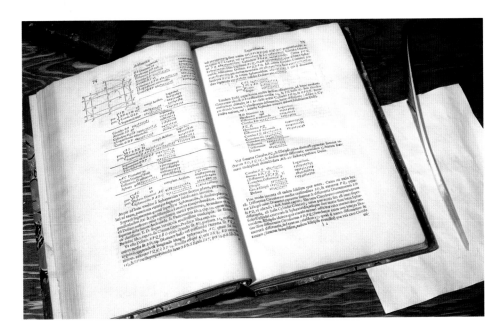

Pages of logarithmic calculations from Henry Briggs' 1624 masterwork *Arithmetica Logarithmica*. Briggs was the first Gresham Professor of Geometry in London and the first Savilian Professor of Geometry at Oxford. Briggs' advocacy of Napier's discovery of logarithms led to the immediate adoption of this new aid to calculation by other mathematical practitioners. He suggested the decimal base instead of Napier's base of $e = 2.717$, and undertook the work of calculating and preparing the tables, which extended to the fourteenth decimal place. Logarithms made the manipulation of large calculations simpler by adding or subtracting the index of two numbers and looking up the result in tables. *(Science Museum.)*

too ill to construct new tables. An observer at their first meeting recorded: 'He brings Mr Briggs into my Lord's chamber, where almost one quarter of an hour was spent, each beholding the other with admiration, before one word was spoken.'

Briggs visited Napier again a year later in 1616, and proceeded to produce and print an extensive series of logarithms. His *Arithmetica Logarithmica* (1624) was printed in Gouda, Holland, a year after his death and published two years later in London under the title *Trigonometria Britannica*. This work remained in general use until the early nineteenth century.

In the later stages of his life Briggs became a Fellow of Merton College, Oxford, where a fellow Halifax man, Sir Henry Savile, was warden. Sir Henry, of Bradley Hall, made him the first Savilian Professor of Geometry at Oxford. Briggs' immense range of interests is demonstrated by his publications on Euclid, geometry, arithmetic, navigation and even the elusive Northwest Passage, about which he was consulted by the Virginia Company.

Briggs' contemporaries saw him as a modest, courteous Puritan and an amiable fellow except when astrology was discussed. Obviously another down-to-earth Yorkshireman. Among the tributes by his peers on his death was this:

'Great Briggs who raced with stars, engirdled earth,
Euclid and Ptolemy in one matched not his worth.'

Sir George Cayley

1773-1857

The founder of the science of aerodynamics who defined the fundamentals of heavier-than-air flight a century before the Wright brothers.

It is now just over 100 years since the Wright brothers shrank the globe with their first heavier-than-air powered flight. But they readily acknowledged they would not have got off the ground but for an amazing Yorkshire baronet — Sir George Cayley, from Scarborough. A century before the Wrights, he defined the fundamentals of flight, and fifty years later his coachman briefly

right Brompton Hall, in the village of Brompton-by-Sawdon near Scarborough. Formerly the ancestral home of George Cayley, it is now a school. *(Photo by Iain Mann.)*

facing page A portrait of Sir George Cayley (1840, oil on canvas) by Henry Perronet Briggs. *(Courtesy National Portrait Gallery, London.)*

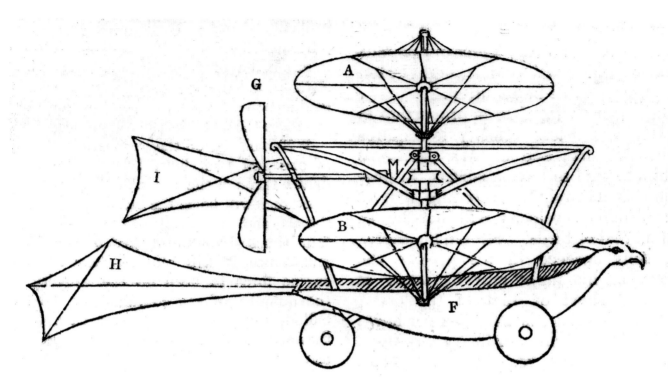

Sir George Cayley, amateur scientist and aviation pioneer, was responsible for designing the first man-carrying glider. In 1808, he constructed and flew a glider with a wing area of 300 square feet, probably the first practical heavier-than-air flying machine. This image shows his innovative 'Aerial Carriage' of 1843, illustrated in the *Mechanics Magazine*. It incorporated four circular discs that were designed to raise the machine vertically, rather like a helicopter, whereupon they were to form circular wings. This ambitious design was never actually built, but remains an example of Cayley's remarkable understanding of the principles of flight. (*Science Museum Library.*)

piloted the Cayley glider on his estate at Brompton — the first heavier-than-air manned flight.

Cayley spent most of his childhood at Helmsley until his father inherited the title and estate at Brompton-by-Sawdon. His mother, a powerful influence over his religious and social beliefs, was a descendant of Robert Bruce. At nineteen, when his father died, he became anything but the stereotyped country squire. He continued his studies, married the daughter of a tutor, and took life and his responsibilities seriously. He became the first landowner to give his tenants land for their own use and was briefly an MP from 1832. After three years he decided he preferred his estate and experiments.

It is thought that the Montgolfier hot-air balloon flight of 1783 caught his childhood imagination. He studied airship travel and ornithopters (flapping wings) but, against the fashion, concentrated on heavier-than-air machines. His first known experiment — and he meticulously recorded his early work — fashioned a working toy helicopter with bird feathers and a bow and string to provide power. He thus demonstrated before the end of the eighteenth century that heavier-than-air flight was possible.

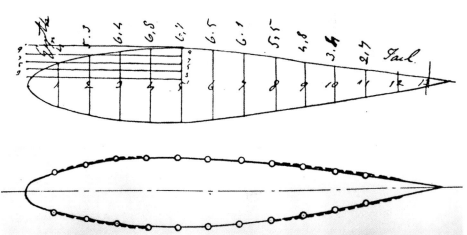

above Sir George Cayley's 1837 design for a navigable balloon. In 1817, Sir George began designing airships, and was the first to recognise that the success of a controllable balloon depended upon the development of an engine with a high power-to-weight ratio. *(Science Museum.)*

left A comparison between Sir George Cayley's wing design (top) and the cross-section of a modern aerofoil shows that they are almost identical. *(Reproduced by kind permission of the Yorkshire Air Museum, Elvington, York.)*

right Inside the main hall of the Regent Street Polytechnic, London. Cayley was heavily involved with the founding in 1838 of this institution dedicated to the dissemination of scientific ideas. *(Reproduced by kind permission of the Yorkshire Air Museum, Elvington, York.)*

below Cayley's toy helicopter, which he built from bird feathers, string and a whalebone bow in 1796. He describes winding up the string and holding the model firmly down with a finger, then 'taking it away suddenly, the machine will rise to the ceiling'. *(Reproduced by kind permission of the Yorkshire Air Museum, Elvington, York.)*

facing page The Cayley Glider replica, built at BAE Systems, Brough, in 2003 and based on the 1852 Governable Parachute plans, is pulled into the air at Brompton Dale, the site of the original glider flight 150 years earlier. *(Photo by Iain Mann.)*

By 1809 he had defined the central problem of flight and described the fundamental principles of an aeroplane. His sketches of wings, based on the streamlining of a trout, are almost identical to modern aerofoils. He experimented with expanding air and gunpowder-propelled machines, and only the lack of suitable propulsion prevented him from attempting powered flight.

In the course of his innovative life, he reclaimed flood plain and researched rail safety. He anticipated the modern bicycle wheel by inventing the tension wheel, the military tank by inventing the caterpillar track to prevent farm machinery getting stuck in heavy ground, and the seat belt. He also designed an artificial hand for the son of a tenant that allowed the man to lift five stones in weight; suggested the self-righting lifeboat; invented a new type of pen nib and an anenometer; and offered a new design for the Covent Garden Theatre when it was burned down.

He was the driving force behind the foundation of the Regent Street Polytechnic to demonstrate scientific principles, and a founder member of the Scarborough Philosophic Society and the York Mechanics' Institute.

He tried three times to form an aeronautical society between 1817 and 1840, but was not taken seriously. He acknowledged he was thought a bit of a crank when he admitted that the subject 'bordered on the ludicrous in public estimation'. But he did not give up. He returned to experiments after his seventieth birthday and constructed a triplane which floated a boy off the ground as it descended a hill. By now, as he worked up to the culmination of his aeronautical research and development, he was becoming pretty dangerous to live with. Four years before his death, his 'new flyer' floated across Brompton Dale. When his coachman-pilot emerged from the infernal machine he was reported to have said: 'Please, Sir George, I wish to give notice. I was hired to drive not to fly'.

Sir John Cockcroft

1897-1967

facing page Nuclear physicist Sir John Cockcroft in 1955 at the Atomic Energy Research Establishment, Harwell, where he was appointed its first director in 1946. *(Photo by Slim Aarons/Getty Images.)*

Todmorden, a former cotton town deep in Yorkshire's Pennine border with Lancashire, has an astonishing claim to fame for a place of only 13,500 souls. It has not one but two Nobel Prize winners. What's more, both went to the same grammar school and, twenty-five years apart, had the same physics master, a certain Luke Sutcliffe. One of them split the atom and the other opened up a new area of chemistry with wide industrial application. The nuclear scientist was Sir John Cockcroft and the inorganic chemist was Sir Geoffrey Wilkinson.

I shall, of course, be accused of prejudice in choosing Cockcroft as the greatest of Yorkshire's seven Nobel prize winners (listed on page 79) because he presented me with my shorthand prize at Todmorden Technical College in the late 1940s. But Cockcroft was the first, with his joint Nobel winner, the Irishman, Professor E T S Walton, to create an artificial nuclear reaction without radioactive substances. He went on to build Britain's nuclear power industry which, for all its temporary unpopularity, is seen as the only way of maintaining global economic development without polluting the atmosphere with greenhouse gases.

Cockcroft came from a family of cotton manufacturers. He survived the First World War in the artillery to study mathematics and electrical engineering in Manchester before taking the mathematical tripos at St John's College, Cambridge, in 1924. He then worked in the Cavendish Laboratory at Cambridge under Lord Rutherford, who laid the groundwork for nuclear physics.

In 1928, Cockcroft turned with Walton to bombarding atoms with a particle accelerator they designed, and they made their atom-splitting breakthrough

Left to right: Dr Ernest Walton, Lord Rutherford (Nobel Prize winner for chemistry in 1908) and Dr John Cockcroft, who together split the atom in 1932 as a result of their research at the Cavendish Laboratory, Cambridge. Cockcroft and Walton later won the 1951 Nobel Prize for physics for their work. *(Photo by Central Press/Getty Images.)*

in 1932. Cockcroft subsequently took charge of the Royal Society Mond Laboratory at Cambridge where he was also Jacksonian Professor of Natural Philosophy in 1939.

Like so many of our brightest scientists, he worked on radar during the Second World War, before going to Canada in 1944 to take charge of the Canadian atomic energy project, where Geoffrey Wilkinson also worked. He then came home in 1946 to direct the UK Atomic Energy Research Establishment at Harwell, and build up the British nuclear industry for both civil and

military purposes. He was elected Master of the new Churchill College at Cambridge in 1959.

Receiving the Nobel Prize in Stockholm at the depth of the Cold War in 1951, he acknowledged that many wished the nuclear genie could be put back in its bottle and blamed science 'for the troubles of our time'. But, he said, 'the overwhelming evil and danger comes not from science but from political ideas which reject the freedom of the human spirit and the values and rights of individual human beings'.

Model of the Cockcroft/Walton research laboratory at Cambridge in the 1930s. John Cockcroft made his name as a physicist through a brilliant experiment with Dr Ernest Walton. They directed accelerated protons at a lithium target, and found that alpha particles were produced. The first artificially induced nuclear reaction had occurred. (*Science Museum.*)

A friend, unveiling a plaque in his memory at Todmorden Town Hall, said: 'His capacity for hard and continuous work was phenomenal, his tenacity of purpose enormous, his courage when things went wrong outstanding … his integrity absolute'.

Todmorden lies in my native upper Calder Valley. And, almost incredibly, that valley claims Yorkshire's seventh Nobel Prize winner, John E Walker (see below). There must be something in its water.

Yorkshire's other Nobel Prize winners are:

Physics, 1928: Sir Owen Willans Richardson (1879-1959), from Dewsbury, for his work on electron emission by hot metals, the principle used in vacuum tubes, leading to his equation, called Richardson's Law, which became an important aid in electronic tube research and technology.

Physics, 1947: Sir Edward V Appleton (1892-1965), from Bradford, for his radio investigations of the physics of the upper atmosphere and especially for the discovery of the so-called Appleton layer, or ionosphere; but for Appleton's work, radar would have come too late to have been of decisive use in the Battle of Britain.

Chemistry, 1967: (jointly with two others) Sir George (later Lord) Porter (1920-2002), from Stainforth near Settle, for studies of extremely fast chemical reactions caused by very short pulses of energy; he was best known as the director of the Royal Institution of Great Britain and for his popular festive season broadcast lectures.

Chemistry, 1973: (jointly with another) Sir Geoffrey Wilkinson (1921-96), from Springside, Todmorden, for pioneering work on the chemistry of organometallic, so-called sandwich, compounds.

Physics, 1977: (jointly with two others) Sir Nevil F Mott (1905-96), from Leeds, for fundamental theoretical investigations of the magnetic and electrical properties of non-crystalline solids — materials widely used in such machines as tape recorders, electronic computers and solar energy converters.

Chemistry, 1997: (jointly with another) John E Walker (1941-), from Halifax, for DNA research elucidating enzymatic mechanisms, giving new insights into how adenosine triphosphate (ATP) is made in the biological world.

facing page The fireball of an H-bomb explosion after a test blast over Bikini Atoll in 1956. Cockcroft argued that the negative aspects of nuclear power and the Cold War 'come not from science but from political ideas'. *(Photo by Time Life Pictures/ Department Of Defense (DOD)/ Time Life Pictures/Getty Images.)*

Sir Fred Hoyle

1915-2001

One of the most creative and provocative astrophysicists of the twentieth century — joint author of the steady state theory of the universe who loved rows, especially with the 'big bang' theorists.

right Fred Hoyle aged ten in his home town of Bingley. He lived at 4 Milnerfield Villas, at the top of a hill in Gilstead. *(By permission of the Master and Fellows of St John's College, Cambridge.)*

facing page Astronomer, scientist and writer Sir Fred Hoyle at home in Bournemouth in December 1994. He coined the term 'big bang' to describe the creation of the cosmos. Sir Fred also put forward the Panspermia Theory, which suggests that life, or the building blocks of life, could be carried to planets by comets or drifting interstellar dust particles. He died on the 20th August 2001 aged eighty-six. *(Photo by David Levenson/Getty Images.)*

Three hundred years ago Jonathan Swift said: 'When a true genius appears in the world, you may know him by this sign, that the dunces are in confederacy against him.' On this basis, Sir Fred Hoyle, from Bingley, amply qualified as a genius — except that the confederacy against him never wore the dunce's cap. It comprised a host of eminent scientists, for Hoyle polarised opinion and relished intellectual combat. Yet he is acknowledged to be one of the most creative as well as provocative astrophysicists since 1945.

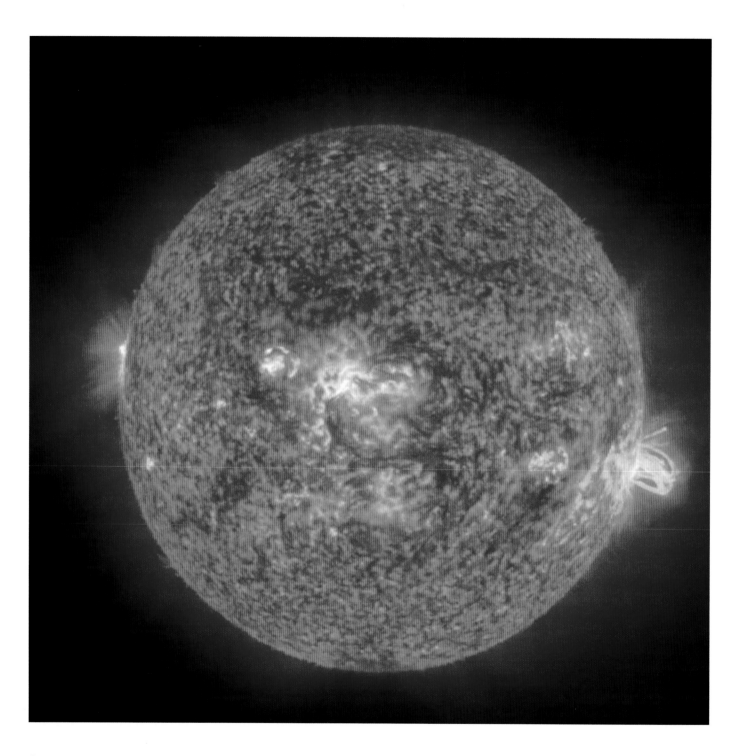

Like most Yorkshiremen, he was born awkward. He found school boring and preferred to study chemistry at home where, alarmingly, he conducted explosive experiments with gunpowder. Fortunately for his family of modest means, he won a scholarship to Bingley Grammar School and went on to read maths at Cambridge. Aged twenty-four, on the outbreak of war, he became a Fellow of St John's College. During the war he led an Admiralty radar research group that included two refugees from Vienna, Thomas Gold and Hermann Bondi. They worked on radar during the day and discussed astrophysics at night.

This very bright trio could not accept that the universe had a beginning and presumably an end. Instead, they developed their 'steady state' theory of the universe, which holds that it is expanding and that matter is continuously being created to keep a constant density in space. It launched a tremendous row with supporters of what Hoyle sarcastically — and memorably — called the 'big bang' theory. He had a genius for the soundbite, too.

Later in life, in concert with Professor Chandra Wickramasinghe, head of mathematics at University College, Wales, he became convinced that life exists throughout the universe, and that bacteria and viruses carried by comets bring life to Earth. By extension, he claimed that sunspots cause flu and other epidemics. More furious argument was engendered by their claim that Darwin's theory of evolution by natural selection was wrong and that evolution is caused by mutating life forms continually falling from space. Hoyle maintained that he proceeded to theorise only from observation, though his theory is not widely accepted.

His work with three others helped to formulate theories about the origins of stars and the origins of metals within them. In a long career showered with honours over sixty years, his serious scientific work inspired three generations of astronomers. He continually sought to answer the biggest questions in science — how did the universe originate and life begin?

In pursuit of the answers, he became a Fellow of the Royal Society in his early forties, and was Plumian Professor of Astronomy and Experimental Philosophy (fourteen years) and director of the Institute of Theoretical Astronomy (five years) until 1972 when he fell out with Cambridge. He was one of the greatest popularisers of science since H G Wells and never wanted for an audience. He became a prolific and masterly science fiction writer, partly with his son, Geoffrey. His *A for Andromeda* became a TV series.

His epitaph might be: 'An uncomfortable genius and fearless searcher after truth whose logic disturbed the finest minds. He had no end of mischievous fun.'

facing page This NASA image from August 2004 shows a solar flare (right) erupting from a giant sunspot. The powerful explosion hurled a coronal mass ejection into space and directed it towards Earth. Sir Fred Hoyle's belief that sunspots cause epidemics on Earth was not popular with his scientific contemporaries. *(HO/AFP/ Getty Images.)*

Sir Almroth Edward Wright

1861-1947

The pioneer immunologist who had a profound impact on the death toll of the First World War and whose aide, Sir Alexander Fleming, discovered penicillin to the immense benefit of mankind.

Sir Almroth Edward Wright in 1929.
(Evening Standard/Getty Images.)

He was single-minded in his pursuit of immunisation. He took no prisoners in argument. His first name, which he acquired from his mother, led his enemies to describe him 'Sir Almost Wright' and 'Sir Always Wrong'. But heaven only knows what the death toll would have been on the Western Front in the First World War but for Sir Edward Wright. And just think how our post-Second World War lives have been transformed by the discovery of penicillin by his long-term aide and colleague, Sir Alexander Fleming.

Wright, born at Middleton Tyas, near Scotch Corner, was one of five able sons of an Irish Evangelical Protestant clergyman. He simultaneously read for degrees in modern languages and medicine at Trinity College, Dublin, but had no idea what to do with his life. Fortunately for the troops, his professor of literature advised him to stick with medicine, even though he had secured a first with gold medal in languages.

It took ten years for him to get his career under way. When the scholarship money for studying physiology in Leipzig ran out, he took a law studentship but never qualified. He passed the Higher Civil Service exams and became an Admiralty clerk for two undemanding years before turning to pathology demonstration at Cambridge University. Then came more study in Germany before becoming a demonstrator in physiology at Sydney University. His wife was unhappy there, so back he came in 1891 to a temporary job at the research laboratories of the Royal College of Physicians and Surgeons. He was in luck.

The superintendent recommended him for the chair of pathology at the Army Medical School. The bacteriologist was on his way. He pursued immunity

British tommies relaxing and having wounds treated in an underground forward dressing station by the Menin Road, France, during the First World War. It was due to Almroth Wright's research that this war was the first in which fewer British soldiers died of infection than missiles. *(Photo by Three Lions/Getty Images.)*

by using himself as a guinea pig. He made himself ill for months with a vaccine for brucellosis, and then was one of eighteen volunteers, some of whom suffered unpleasant side-effects, in recording active immunisation against typhoid.

He became so disenchanted with the army that he was prepared in 1902 to join St Mary's Hospital Medical School for less than half the salary as a pathologist and bacteriologist. He was to remain there for the rest of his life, developing the science of immunology, and in the early years so poverty-stricken that microscopy in his room was impossible because of the vibration from the London Underground. He still managed to develop vaccines against enteric tuberculosis and pneumonia, and study opsonins, blood enzymes that help to kill off bacteria.

He worked with Alexander Fleming for forty years, and both went to France in the First World War to tackle the problem of gas gangrene that was such a scourge of trench warfare. That was after he had campaigned for and badgered Lord Kitchener into introducing compulsory anti-typhoid immunisation. The incidence of typhoid on the Western Front was negligible compared with the deaths of 9,000 men from it in the more limited Boer War.

For all his force of personality, penchant for argument and eccentricity, he commanded the loyalty of a distinguished staff. They recognised what he was about: serving humanity. St Mary's Inoculation Department became the Wright-Fleming Institute, and his campaign for central funding for medical research eventually led to the formation of the Medical Research Council.

Amy Johnson

1903-41

The jilted girl who found solace in flying and as 'Amy, wonderful Amy' became an international celebrity as she claimed long-distance flying records during aviation's infancy.

right The pioneering aviator Amy Johnson flying her plane *The Seafarer* in 1932. *(Photo by Hulton Archive/ Getty Images.)*

facing page A portrait of Amy Johnson (oil on canvas, *circa* 1930) by Sir John Longstaff. The daughter of a Hull herring importer, Amy Johnson trained as a secretary, but developed a consuming passion for flying. With no more experience than a flight from London to Hull, on the 5th May 1930 she set out to fly solo to Australia in a tiny Gipsy Moth and landed in Port Darwin nineteen days later. Though not a record time, her flight was an astonishing achievement and aroused universal enthusiasm. *(Courtesy National Portrait Gallery, London.)*

Just after the First World War, two former RAF pilots landed a battered Avro 504 biplane in a field near Hull, offering flights at five bob a time. Amy Johnson and her sister, daughters of a fish merchant, pooled their money and flew for the first time. 'Oh, the disappointment!' Amy wrote later. 'There was no sensation. Just a lot of noise and wind, smell of burnt oil and escaping petrol … I was almost — not quite — cured of flying for ever'.

AMY JOHNSON

She might well have been cured had she not been jilted by a Swiss chap. After keeping her on a string for nearly ten years, he married another. She found solace in learning to fly at the London Aeroplane Club near her home in Hendon. The Sheffield University arts graduate had escaped a life blighted in her native Hull by her wait for a marriage proposal to work initially at Peter Jones in Sloane Square and then in an informal legal apprenticeship in the City.

She was always rebellious, restless and liberated, but never a natural flyer. It took her twice as long as was typical to go solo. She got her pilot's licence in July 1929 and then became the first British woman to qualify as a ground engineer. Six months later, the compleat aviator told a journalist of her plan to challenge the solo flight record of fifteen days from England to Australia. The massive publicity helped her to win the financial backing of Lord Wakefield.

Less than two months after passing her navigation exam, she set out in her De Havilland Gipsy Moth, *Jason*, from Croydon on the 5th May 1930 with only seventy-five hours of flying time behind her. 'The prospect did not frighten me', she said later, 'because I was so appallingly ignorant that I never realised in the least what I had taken on'.

She soon did. No radio, no maps other than those bought in shops, rudimentary weather forecasts, pot luck with airfields, the right fuel and spares along the way, and the perpetual reek of petrol. She nearly ran into a ravine in the Taurus

Pioneering aviator Amy Johnson with her biplane in 1939. *(Rex Features.)*

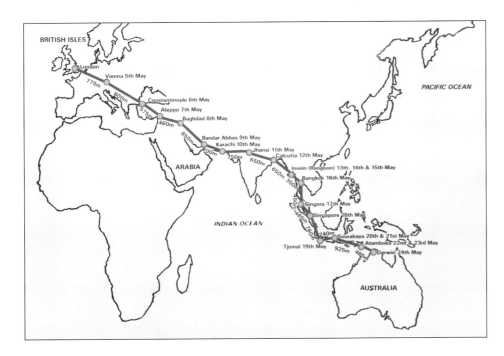

In the map, the following labels appear:

BRITISH ISLES
London
Vienna 5th May
775m
800m
Constantinople 6th May
575m
Aleppo 7th May
460m
Baghdad 8th May
850m
Bandar Abbas 9th May
Karachi 10th May
700m
750m
Jhansi 11th May
650m
Calcutta 12th May
ARABIA
650m
350m
Insein (Rangoon) 13th, 14th & 15th May
Bangkok 16th May
INDIAN OCEAN
465m
Singora 17th May
Singapore 18th May
240m
Sourabaya 20th & 21st May
Tjomal 19th May
925m
485m
Atamboea 22nd & 23rd May
Darwin 24th May
AUSTRALIA
PACIFIC OCEAN

In May 1930, Amy Johnson became the first woman to fly solo from England to Australia, winning £10,000 from the *Daily Mail*. Her plane was a De Havilland Gipsy Moth (nicknamed 'Jason'). In 1932, she set a record for the fastest solo flight from England to Cape Town, and broke that record four years later. In 1933, with her husband James Mollison, she flew in a De Havilland biplane non-stop across the Atlantic in thirty-nine hours. She joined the Air Transport Auxiliary as a pilot in the Second World War, during which she was lost after baling out over the Thames Estuary. *(Science Museum.)*

Mountains in Turkey, made a forced landing in a sandstorm in Iraq and crash-landed near Rangoon, after which her plane was pulled by a fire engine twelve miles to the racecourse for take-off. She reached Darwin on Empire Day, four days too late for the record. But the *Daily Mail* awarded her £10,000, 'the largest amount ever paid for a feat of daring', and she was congratulated by the King and Prime Minister. In the words of a popular song she was 'Amy, wonderful Amy'.

Hull's most famous daughter then tried to fly across Siberia to China in 1931 but crash-landed near Warsaw. Later that year, with the man who taught her engineering as co-pilot, she beat the record for a light plane from Berlin to Tokyo. In 1932 she cut eleven hours off the solo record from London to Cape Town set up by her Scottish-born husband, Jim Mollison, and recovered it again in 1936. In 1933 the newly-weds took off from Wales for New York, and ended up in hospital when they overshot the runway in Connecticut after Mollison had refused to refuel in Boston.

She was never lucky in love and soon divorced. Nor could she find a regular job in aviation to maintain her hedonistic lifestyle. Eventually the Second World War brought her a job ferrying planes for the Air Transport Auxiliary. Ironically, after her 2,300 hours in the air, she vanished over the Thames Estuary in 1941. Her body was never found.

Baroness Boothroyd

1929-

The 155th Speaker of the House of Commons was not the first from Yorkshire. John Henry Whitley (1921-28) was a distinguished predecessor — a Halifax man who lent his name to the joint industrial councils he recommended after the First World War to improve industrial relations. But Betty Boothroyd is in this book because she is the first woman to take the Speaker's chair. Her breakthrough — and success — consolidated Margaret Thatcher's spectacular achievement in becoming Britain's first woman Prime Minister.

Baroness (as she now is) Boothroyd never set her sights on the Speakership any more than Lady Thatcher ever thought (until she became Tory leader) there would be a woman Prime Minister in her time. Instead, she was stage-struck. With a big voice and some lovely legs for dancing, first exercised as principal boy in local pantomimes, she entertained the troops for ENSA across Yorkshire as a member of a teenage jazz band, the Swing Stars.

Her father fought her determination to be a professional dancer. At seventeen she joined the John Tiller School in London in the fierce winter of 1946-7, and briefly appeared at the London Palladium and with the Skyrockets. But a foot infection in pantomime at Luton enabled her to escape the privations of a world into which she did not fit. She returned to her home and birthplace, 24 Marriott Street, Dewsbury, to recover from the setback and begin preparing, as it turned out, to adorn a much larger stage.

Her materially impoverished working-class upbringing is familiar to millions of her generation: her father's unemployment, her eleven-plus failure, an office job — the summit of her parents' ambition for her — and Labour

Betty Boothroyd photographed by Lord Snowdon on the occasion of her retirement in October 2000 as speaker of the House of Commons, a post she held for eight years. *(Photograph by Snowdon, Camera Press London.)*

Labour candidate Betty Boothroyd outside the houses of Parliament on the 31st October 1957. Boothroyd, an ex-Tiller Girl, later became the first woman Speaker of the House of Commons. *(Photo by Evening Standard/Getty Images.)*

allegiance. Her remarkable mother took her to Labour rallies from an early age and, with dancing behind her, she began to enjoy the Labour League of Youth. She became Yorkshire's representative on its national committee and in 1952 won its national speaking award, judged by Denis Healey. She was really bitten by the political bug that year when she narrowly lost a Dewsbury council election in a hopeless ward.

Soon she was working for the party's research department at its Transport House headquarters, and then as secretary to two Labour MPs at different ends of the political spectrum — Geoffrey de Freitas and Barbara Castle.

He mind was broadened by travel, secondment to offices of Democrat senators in Washington DC and a long tenure as personal/political assistant to Lord Walston, a Labour landowner whose homes near Cambridge and in St Lucia were socialist salons. If these were the years of social grooming and confidence building, they were also frustrating. She lost elections in four seats — Leicester SE, Peterborough and North Northants, Nelson and Colne, and Rossendale — before her proud mother saw her win West Bromwich in 1973. In 1987 she became a deputy Speaker — 'Call me Madam', she told an MP who inquired how to address her — and Speaker in 1992 with a landslide majority.

Her eight years in the Speaker's chair recall the TV image of a comely and authoritative woman who forsook the traditional full-bottomed wig for her own ample 'thatch', bringing proceedings to a close with a barmaid's 'Time's up'. The substance behind the image is of a Yorkshire lass whose defence of MPs' rights commanded the support of the House through John Major's fractious decline and fall, and the worst of Tony Blair's sidelining of Parliament. I think I know why, when she retired, she told MPs: 'Be happy for me'.

We can justifiably be very happy for her. She is proud of her chancellorship of the Open University, and 2005 brought her more real senses of achievement. After sixty years she secured recognition of the role of women in the Second World War. As patron of the Yorkshire-based Women of World War II Memorial Trust, she saw the Queen unveil a monument in Whitehall, London, to the contribution of 7.1 million women to the successful war effort. Earlier the Queen had bestowed upon her the Order of Merit.

The Bradford-born artist David Hockney with the speaker of the House of Commons Betty Boothroyd after both received honorary degrees from Oxford University on the 21st June 1995. *(Photograph by Graham Wiltshire, Camera Press London.)*

Second Marquis of Rockingham

1730-82

Herbert Henry Asquith

1852-1928

James Harold Wilson

1916-95

Yorkshire has contributed three Prime Ministers to the nation's governance. Between them they illustrate the social evolution of our political leaders — from the landed gent of Rockingham, through the barrister Asquith, the first from the professional middle classes, to the economist and statistician Wilson, the first technocrat in No 10 Downing Street.

They were all liberal in outlook but none can be regarded as an outstanding Prime Minister, though each left his mark on politics and the nation. Indeed, the Rockingham Whigs, who opposed Britain's war against the American colonists, are seen as the first manifestation of a modern political party with a programme they sought to carry through in office.

Asquith and Wilson pose two conundrums: what was in Huddersfield's industrial atmosphere; and what peculiar political gifts did the Congregational Church bestow on its northern sons? Both were born into Congregational families and both first went to school in Huddersfield. Accordingly, I shall look at Asquith and Wilson together, and Rockingham separately.

Wilson was born in Cowersley, Huddersfield, a few months before Asquith, born in Morley, was forced out of No 10 by the more charismatic and dynamic Lloyd George in the middle of the First World War. Wilson's education began at New Street Council School in Milnsbridge. Asquith went briefly to Huddersfield College when his maternal grandfather took responsibility for educating him and his elder brother on their father's death when he was seven. Their different schools sixty years apart reflect their differing social status —

Morley's contribution to the governance of Britain: Herbert Henry Asquith, first Earl of Oxford and Asquith, portrayed in 1919 by André Cluysenaar. Asquith, the imperialist free trader and Irish home ruler who laid the foundations of the welfare state, led the nation into the First World War and presided unflappably over the last great days of the Liberal Party. *(By courtesy of the National Portrait Gallery, London.)*

October 1908: from left to right, Mr J A Pease (Lord Gainford), British prime minister Herbert Henry Asquith, First Viscount Haldane, Mr McKenna and First Viscount Samuel in the House of Commons. Mr Asquith is delivering a speech on events in the Balkans during the Turkish Revolution. Drawn by Ralph Gleaver for the *Graphic*. *(Photo by Hulton Archive/Getty Images)*

Wilson the only son of an industrial chemist too often unemployed, and Asquith from a millowner's comfortable home.

Both went on to brilliant academic careers at Oxford — Asquith, the star classicist of Balliol, and Wilson the glittering PPE first at the more down-market Jesus. Both were dons before becoming serious politicians. Asquith sat for East Fife for thirty-two years, led the Liberal Party for eighteen years and was Prime Minister for nearly nine. Wilson was MP for Ormskirk or Huyton on the edge of Merseyside for thirty-eight years, led the Labour Party for thirteen years, served as Prime Minister for some eight years and, as he often boasted, won — some only 'nobbut just' — four out of the five elections he fought as Prime Minister. Both wrestled with strikes, Irish nationalism and the problems of governments with miniscule or no overall majorities. Both led their parties from left of centre, and both were reformers.

Asquith laid the foundations of the welfare state with the National Insurance Act of 1911, oversaw the Parliament Act of the same year, ending the Lords' veto over financial legislation, and secured royal assent for the Irish Home Rule Bill in 1914, though its operation was suspended for the duration of the First World War.

Wilson expanded higher education and established the Open University, perhaps his proudest achievement. He also presided over a welter of social legislation creating a more open, 'permissive' society and cemented Britain's membership of what is now the European Union with a two to one vote in confirmation of it in a 1975 referendum.

Both Asquith and Wilson liked the company of women, though curiously Asquith was against women's suffrage. Asquith maintained a voluminous correspondence with lady friends, and Wilson was dominated and often burdened, according to officials, by his personal and political secretary, Marcia Williams, later Lady Falkender.

There the similarities end. Asquith struggled for ten years to establish himself at the bar before rising with the effortless ease of the Balliol man through the offices of Home Secretary and Chancellor of the Exchequer under Gladstone, Rosebery and Campbell-Bannerman to No 10. He made it as Prime Minister even though he had to reject the first offer of the Liberal leadership in 1898 for financial reasons.

Wilson made his mark as the researcher for Sir William Beveridge, author of the report that brought the great social welfare reforms after the Second World War. He was then directed into the Civil Service at the beginning of the war and, as director of economics and statistics at the Ministry of Fuel and Power, produced a study of the coalmining industry and later a book, *New Deal for Coal*, which formed the basis for Labour's nationalisation of the mines.

He was an MP by the age of thirty and, as President of the Board of Trade, the youngest member of the Cabinet (in this case Attlee's) since 1806.

Another memorable Wilson image: a photograph of the future Prime Minister posing outside No 10 Downing Street in 1924. *(Photo by Evening Standard/Hulton Archive/ Getty Images)*

Baron Wilson of Rievaulx (1974, oil on canvas) by Ruskin Spear. Harold Wilson was an inveterate pipesmoker, and the author once saw him set his suit alight, having put his pipe in his jacket pocket, outside the Imperial Hotel in Blackpool. Wilson was a technocrat who won four out of five elections as Labour leader; ushered in the permissive society with a raft of social legislation; and wore himself out holding his party together. He was often to be seen wreathed in clouds of smoke, making Spear's portrait so evocative. *(By courtesy of the National Portrait Gallery, London.)*

He resigned from the Government in 1951 over the imposition of NHS charges but emerged as Labour leader on the sudden death of Hugh Gaitskell in 1963. He then promoted the idea of harnessing 'the white heat of the technological revolution' through indicative planning.

Asquith always commanded the Commons, whereas Wilson was initially a most boring performer. Asquith first married a domesticated Manchester woman who died of typhoid, leaving him with five young children. He remarried money in the electric form of Margot Tennant, a hard-riding huntswoman and opinionated political wife, and readily took to the country house life of the gentry with whom he indulged his passion for bridge. Wilson married his first love, Mary, who guarded his domestic privacy. They were the very opposites of the socialite Asquiths.

Asquith was relaxed to a fault, the unflappable exponent of wait-and-see politics. It was his lackadaisical nature of conducting the First World War that forced him into his first coalition and then his replacement by Lloyd George. Wilson, always a bit of a show-off, displayed immense energy in his first period as Prime Minister (1964-70), not to mention ingenuity and cunning. None of his rivals in a fractious administration ever got up quite early enough to outwit him. He saw them all off before resigning of his own volition at sixty to launch a thousand fanciful, not to say scurrilous, theories as to why he went.

Wilson wore himself out on such diverse problems as Rhodesia's unilateral declaration of independence, containing the abuse of trade union power at which his Cabinet baulked, an economy unresponsive to his passion for central planning and, not least, holding his fissiparous party together. The much more measured Asquith was not made to be worn out but had plenty of traumas to endure: leading his nation into a bloody war and, in 1916, his *annus horribilis*, losing his brilliant eldest son on the Somme, misjudging the issue of conscription and Dublin's Easter Rising.

If Labour came close to losing the plot in the 1980s after Wilson departed, the Liberals were never again a potent force after Asquith.

Their connection with Yorkshire ended with their schooling — Asquith when he left the Moravian school at Fulneck for the City of London School, and Wilson when he departed Royds Hall Grammar School, Huddersfield, for the Wirral. They perpetuated their links in their titles: the heir to the Earl of Oxford and Asquith KG became Viscount Asquith of Morley; Lord Wilson of Rievaulx KG took the title from the abbey lands that generations of Wilsons farmed until the mid-nineteenth century.

Charles Watson-Wentworth, 2nd Marquis of Rockingham (1766-8, oil on canvas), after Sir Joshua Reynolds. Watson-Wentworth was the leader of the Rockingham Whigs, the first manifestation of a political party with a programme, who achieved much in two short bursts as Prime Minister, even though he was entirely deficient as an orator. *(By courtesy of the National Portrait Gallery, London.)*

Charles Watson-Wentworth was born in the family home, Wentworth Woodhouse, near Rotherham, that his father built with the longest front of any English country house. He was the fifth son in a family of ten and, as the only son to survive to childhood, was heir to vast estates and the Whig leadership in Yorkshire. His education is somewhat uncertain — Eton or Westminster and possibly St John's, Cambridge. But at the age of fifteen he became a colonel in his father's regiment of volunteers at Pontefract, raised to meet Bonnie Prince Charlie's threatened invasion. He must have been an adventurous lad because, to get nearer the enemy, he rode in winter to Carlisle to join the Duke of Cumberland. It was the start of a lifelong friendship that was to make him Prime Minister.

After the excitements of 1745, Rockingham was packed off on the Grand Tour to get the idea of a military career out of his system. He was abroad when his father died in 1750. He took his seat in the Lords, where he spent his entire political career, married a sixteen year old for love at twenty-two, and settled down to national and Yorkshire responsibilities, and his estates. He was a caring, accessible landlord, giving long leases to Roman Catholics, remitting or reducing rents in hard times and improving homes. He was also a good employer to Wentworth's huge staff and farmworkers, and boosted the local economy with such schemes as an £85,000 stable block at Wentworth. As Lord Lieutenant of Yorkshire, responsible for law and order, he defended Hull and the East Coast from American privateers, and brought to book the Cragg Vale coiners who made a business of clipping gold coins in Halifax.

He was Gentleman of the Bedchamber to George II and George III, and was made a Knight of the Garter in 1760. Two years later he lost his appointments under the Massacre of the Pelhamite Innocents — the wholesale removal of office holders to break the grip of the Whig Grandees. But you can't keep a good man with high principles down. In 1776 Cumberland was asked to form a new ministry and made Rockingham his First Lord of the Treasury — ie Prime Minister. This ministry lasted only a year because of internal dissension, but in that year Rockingham tackled the colonial problem by repealing the hated Stamp Act, though only at the price of another law declaring Parliament's right to make laws binding on the colonies.

For the next sixteen years Rockingham was in opposition supporting the colonies, and demanding Parliamentary reform and religious tolerance. Then, as leader of the largest group in Parliament, the king had no option in 1782 but to recall him. In the fourteen weeks before his death from flu, this remarkable

man, entirely deficient as an orator, initiated peace negotiations with the American colonists, secured legislative independence for the Irish parliament and limited the king's patronage. Edmund Burke said of him: '…he did not live for himself. He far exceeded all other statesmen in the art of drawing together, without the seduction of self-interest, the concurrence and co-operation of various dispositions and abilities of men.'

The east side of Wentworth Woodhouse is the longest country-house frontage in the country. This was the family home of Charles Watson-Wentworth, who was the first Prime Minister from Yorkshire, born here in 1730. *(Photo by Chris Craggs.)*

Sir Titus Salt
1803-76

The worsted entrepreneur whose creation — the village of Saltaire — is an international monument to capitalism's noblest objective: the improvement of working men and women.

Corporate social responsibility is all the rage these days — or at least it is good for a pious passage in company annual reports. Titus Salt practised it 150 years ago. In the process he was one of those who demonstrated how much more this nation owes to Methodism, or Nonconformism, than Marx. He wasn't the first West Yorkshire capitalist to show practical concern for his workpeople and the community, but he was the most spectacularly successful.

His model village at Saltaire — named after him and the river on whose banks he relocated his mills — is a monument to his social concern. His mills were rescued from dereliction by another entrepreneur, the late Jonathan

right The decorative letterhead for Salts Mill shows the mill buildings constructed in the early 1850s. A second 'new mill' was added in 1868, with a chimney copying the campanile of the Venetian church of Santamaria Gloriosa. *(Dorothy Burrows.)*

facing page The textile manufacturer Titus Salt *circa* 1870. He joined the family wool business in Bradford in 1824, and developed it into a major company. Later he built the model village of Saltaire, the most modern industrial community in Europe, with housing for workers, fresh water and gas. *(Hulton Archive/Getty Images.)*

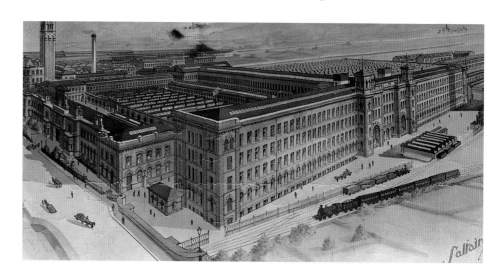

The textile industry gradually declined during the twentieth century, and by the 1980s Salts Mill had become virtually redundant. Eventually Jonathan Silver purchased the mill in 1987. It was semi-derelict and appeared to have no future. But, through Jonathan's vision and determination, Salts Mill was transformed into modern office space, shops selling everything from outdoor clothing to designer jewellery, a restaurant and theatre space, and the 1853 Hockney Gallery (pictured). Over 1,500 people are employed on the site by firms which include large hi-tech manufacturing companies like Pace Electronics and Filtronic Comtek. Since Jonathan died in 1997, his wife Maggie has taken on the formidable yet challenging task of taking Salts Mill into the twenty-first century. *(Photo by Mike Kipling.)*

Silver, in 1987 to become an awarding-winning cultural and hi-tech manufacturing centre with David Hockney's works extensively on show.

The Salts originated in Staffordshire and plied their trades northwards to iron founding in Hunslet, Leeds. Titus's father married into drysalting at Morley, where Titus was born, the first child, into a deeply religious home. A sturdy, well-built lad, he was educated at a Morley dame school, then in Batley — a round trip of six miles — and finally at a chapel day school in Wakefield, since his father had by then become a farmer at Crofton. Titus and his sister rode to school on a donkey.

At seventeen he was set to learn wool-stapling — that is, the wool trade. Two years later he went to burgeoning Bradford where his father, having failed as a farmer, set up in business in wool, too. Titus completed his wool

An aerial view of the massive mill complex, village and part of the chapel (bottom right) built by Sir Titus Salt. *(Courtesy Salts Mill.)*

The burling and mending department inside Salts Mill. *(Dorothy Burrows.)*

training with Rouse and Son before becoming the driving force in the family firm, a leading light at Horton Lane Congregational Chapel from which, it was said, Bradford was run, and a force for the moral, spiritual and social improvement of the community.

At twenty-seven he married the daughter of a Lincolnshire farmer — a wool grower. And then he gambled. He invested in Donskoi wool from sheep on the banks of the Russian Don, spun and wove it himself, and introduced a new staple to the worsted trade. Another gamble followed. Charles Dickens told how Salt took 300 bales of alpaca wool from Peru off the hands of a grateful Liverpool merchant and, after months of experiment, brought yet another fibre to the worsted trade. The Salt business took off on the back of alpaca, and so did the taciturn Titus Salt's civic work. He became the second mayor of Bradford in 1848 at a time of privation caused by mechanisation, Chartist agitation, riots and hunger.

He had intended to retire at fifty to farm but Salt and Son, operating from five mills, needed to be brought together. Bradford, however, was one of the filthiest towns in the world and was ravaged by cholera in 1849. The idea of moving three miles up the Aire Valley to the pure air near Shipley was born. He opened his first monumental mill in 1853, and over the next twenty-five

The Congregational church built by
Sir Titus Salt in 1868 for the spiritual
sustenance of Saltaire's mill workers is
his most impressive and lasting
architectural achievement.
The interior is a sumptuous and
restrained display of colour and style.
The church also serves as Salt's
personal mausoleum.
(Photo by Mike Kipling.)

A general view from the north-west circa 1865 of Titus Salt's model village (built 1851-71), alpaca and mohair textile mills (1851-2).

years built — all in Yorkshire stone — 823 houses, shops, schools and Sunday schools, baths and wash houses, almshouses and infirmary, club and institute, a Wesleyan chapel, a sumptuous Congregational church and a park.

He was briefly Liberal MP for Bradford and a philanthropist on a grand scale. Paternalist he may have been, but he lavished his wealth on Bradford and elsewhere, and died massively mourned by the nation as well as the West Riding. Sadly, his company survived him by only sixteen years, suffering a severe blow when his son, Titus, died young.

Sir Michael Sadler

1861-1943

A public school radical who became a world authority on education and its improvement.

We have benefited immensely from the Michael Sadlers' social conscience. One led the factory reform movement in the nineteenth century that produced the Factory Act of 1833. His kinsman became a world-renowned authority on secondary education. Yorkshire's hero is the educationist. He was born, the first child of a Barnsley physician, into a radical home through which passed leaders of the working-class movement.

At the age of ten he was 'swung from the Radical West Riding … where I never heard the Conservative point of view properly put … into an entirely new atmosphere in which the old Conservative and Anglican traditions were still strong'. In short, he was packed off to a private boarding school in Winchester and then Rugby, steeped in the Cromwellian Puritan revolution. No Cavalier emerged. At Trinity College, Oxford, he was captured by John Ruskin's concept of social justice.

His first in classics and presidency of the Oxford Union opened up many doors — teaching, the Colonies, journalism and politics. Refusing to be monopolised by any one political party, he opted for adult education. In 1885 he became secretary to Oxford University's standing committee of the delegacy for local examinations, and for nine years was a travelling lecturer, tutor and organiser of lectures for the working classes. He gave them an early assessment of Karl Marx — his 'suggestions of practical reform for the future are not as valuable as his indictment of the past'. Under his leadership these extension courses grew enormously and led to his invitation to speak at an American conference in Philadelphia. There he charted his course for the

Sir Michael Ernest Sadler, photographed by George Charles Beresford in 1914. If ever a man deserved the epitaph conjured up by the modern political slogan 'Education, education, education', it is Sadler. He devoted his life to it. He became a world authority on it, and successively vice-chanceller of Leeds University and master of University College, Oxford. One shudders to think how he would now view the current state of eduction. We need another Sadler *(Courtesy National Portrait Gallery, London.)*

Pupils at South Featherstone Modern School, Purston, Yorkshire, have their heads down over their desks, while others are busy in one of the largest school gardens in England, in July 1939. Teaching methods such as this were due to Sir Michael Sadler's efforts to establish the principle of secondary education for all. *(Photo by Fox Photos/Getty Images.)*

future: 'The next step we have to take in England is that of secondary education, a medium between primary and university'.

He so passionately espoused the cause that he persuaded Oxford to hold the first conference on the development of secondary education. This led to a royal commission on which he served and to his becoming a pioneer of comparative education on an international scale. That led him to challenge the inadequacy of Britain's commercial and industrial training. For his pains he became the first director of the Government's Office of Special Inquiries and Reports. His work between 1895 and 1903 produced eleven volumes of comparative reports on education with the aim of promoting consensus on the development of Britain's system.

Frustrated with political control, he found himself without a job at forty-two after resigning from the Civil Service. Manchester University then made him part-time professor of history and administration of education. This left him with plenty of time to help local authorities reorganise their education after acquiring secondary education powers in 1902. In 1911 he came home, as it were, as vice-chancellor of Leeds University to build up a centre of learning and widen educational opportunities. In twelve years, through the First World War and several years of postwar economic depression and social unrest, he greatly increased its faculty, students and academic stature. For two years he chaired a commission examining Calcutta University that brought thirteen volumes of reports and a knighthood.

Then from 1923 until his retirement in 1934 he became Master of University College, Oxford, where he lectured and worked on a history of English education. He saw the fruits of education as 'an attitude of mind ... toward life, work, duty and the realities of belief. In it are blended freedom and discipline, questioning and awe ... training and self-training, science and letters, preparation for livelihood and leisure alike'. Is Sir Michael now turning in his grave?

A later photograph of Sir Michael Sadler, the energetic and forward-thinking vice-chancellor of Leeds University from 1911 to 1923. *(University of Leeds.)*

John Curwen

1816-80

The Congregational minister who introduced an easy method — the tonic sol-fa system — for teaching children to read music by sight and established a music publishing empire.

Could Rogers and Hammerstein have composed 'Do-Re-Mi' for Julie Andrews to sing in *The Sound of Music* without John Curwen of Heckmondwike? It seems unlikely because the Rev Curwen, a Congregational minister, codified the tonic sol-fa system of naming the pitches of musical notes 100 years before Rogers and Hammerstein had us 'Do-Re-Mi'-ing in 1959.

Curwen did not invent the system. Guido of Arezzo, a Benedictine monk, hit upon the idea more than 1,200 years ago — around 770 AD. He used syllables to represent notes on the scale. He employed the first syllables of the Latin words sung to them, and they came out as ut, re, mi, fa, sol and la. In Italy, ut was changed to doh and si (which ultimately became ti) was added later.

As an enthusiastic young minister in his first pastorate, Curwen recognised the religious value of hymn singing for children in his Sunday school. But he himself had experienced difficulty with reading music at sight from the unadorned score or by staff notation, as it is called. He then discovered a system devised by Sarah Glover (1785-1867) in Norwich, and at the age of twenty-five was commissioned by a conference of Sunday school teachers to introduce and promote a simple way of teaching music to youngsters.

He modified Miss Glover's sol-fa notation for pitch, and devised a simple way of denoting rhythm and emphasis. His aim was to develop musical literacy in three stages: first, reading from sol-fa notation; then reading from the score with the help of sol-fa notation; and finally just from the score. He even invented pitch hand-signs to denote each note on the scale.

John Curwen (oil on canvas, *circa* 1857) by William Gush. It could be said that this handsome chap taught the world to sing — or, more accurately, to sing from sheet music — by introducing the tonic sol-fa system. It is entirely appropriate that he came from a Pennine valley where the choral tradition is part of our culture and is so inspiringly upheld by many choral societies. *(Courtesy National Portrait Gallery, London.)*

His tonic sol-fa method became the principal choral teaching method in Britain in the nineteenth century. It was officially recognised by the English Education Department in 1861 and was widely adopted in the colonies. By 1891, two and a half million children in Britain were receiving tonic sol-fa instruction in elementary schools. If anybody got the country — nay, the world — singing hymns it was John Curwen. Missionaries carried his teaching methods to the extremities of the Empire, and to the USA, China and even Madagascar.

Soon the system became Curwen's life work and business. In 1853 he established the Tonic Sol-Fa College (successively the Curwen Memorial College and then the Curwen Institute) in London. Ten years later he launched J Curwen and Sons, musical publishers for the Tonic Sol-Fa movement, with its own journal, *The Musical Herald*. His publishing firm, eventually known as the Curwen Press, survived to the 1970s. His son, John Spencer Curwen, followed his father as principal of the Tonic Sol-Fa College, which continues to this day as the Curwen Institute, and founded the competitive festival movement in England for amateur musicians.

If Curwen provided an easy method of teaching children (and adults) to read music by sight, it did not commend itself to musicians at large once they had grown out of it. But would chapel choirs of Yorkshire's dales and vales have worshipped the Lord so mellifluously without him? Or Rogers and Hammerstein had a hit? I doubt it. Let us sing the praises of John Curwen. His memorial is in Green Park, Heckmondwike.

General Sir Thomas Fairfax

1612-71

The great commander-in-chief of the Parliamentary army during the English Civil Wars.

'Black Tom', as he was known because of his dark complexion, was interested in Roman antiquities and cultivating roses — a gentle, learned man of principle. But he was also the daring, reckless and strictly disciplinarian commander-in-chief of the victorious Parliamentary army in the English Civil Wars between Royalists and Parliamentarians.

Thomas Fairfax, curious chap that he was, was born the eldest son of Ferdinando, second Baron Fairfax, at Denton, near Ilkley. After St John's College, Cambridge, he gained early campaign experience fighting with the English brigade for the Dutch in the Thirty Years War. He marched with King Charles I against the Scots in the first Bishop's War and was knighted in 1640.

Two years later, while most of the gentry sided with the king, he and his father declared for Parliament. He saw himself fighting for the principles of the *Magna Carta*. His command of the Yorkshire cavalry began badly with defeat at Adwalton Moor in 1643 that left most of Yorkshire under Royalist control. The Fairfaxes then kept the king's forces in the North tied down with guerrilla raids from their redoubt in Hull.

Sir Thomas went on to co-operate with Cromwell in a campaign that restored Parliamentary control of the North with victory at Marston Moor near York, where he commanded the right wing of the Parliamentary army. Most of his officers were wounded in that bloody battle, and he himself suffered serious wounds a few months later in the siege of Helmsley Castle. He recovered sufficiently during the winter to be made commander-in-chief of the New Model Army because he was one of the few Parliamentary commanders

Fairfax the General

Thomas 3rd Lord Fairfax (oil on canvas), in the style of Robert Walker. And what a contradiction Fairfax was. Daring but immensely disciplined in war. Reckless but meticulous in his treatment of civilians. A man of immense integrity. Gentle and learned in peace. A liberal in advance of his times. *(Trustees of Leeds Castle Foundation, Maidstone, Kent; www.bridgeman.co.uk.)*

not affected by an ordinance ruling that membership of either House of Parliament was incompatible with military command.

Fairfax's organisation and training led to the decisive victory over Charles I at Naseby in Northamptonshire in 1645. He then marched triumphantly through the West Country before taking the surrender of the Royalist headquarters at Oxford a year later. The discipline of his army and its treatment of the civilian population contrasted with the plundering and lawlessness of those under Royalist commanders. He sent his Cornish prisoners home with

After the Battle of Naseby in 1645 (1860, watercolour on paper) by Sir John Gilbert. *(Towneley Hall Art Gallery and Museum, Burnley, Lancashire; www.bridgeman.co.uk.)*

Engraving after a painting by Ernest Crofts of Oliver Cromwell leading troops at Marston Moor on the 2nd July 1644. The Parliamentary victory here, inspired in no small part by Sir Thomas Fairfax's military skills, was a decisive moment in the English Civil War. *(Photo by Time Life Pictures/Mansell/Time Life Pictures/Getty Images.)*

two shillings each to spread the word that the Parliamentarians had not come to rob them.

In the Second Civil War, he crushed a Royalist uprising in Kent and starved Colchester into submission. He hoped to see a limited monarchy restored and refused to serve on the commission that condemned Charles I to death. When his name was called out by the court, his spirited wife, daughter of his first commander, cried out: 'He hath more wit than to be here'. Cromwell thought it prudent to detain Fairfax in prayer while the king went to the scaffold lest he tried to stop his execution.

Two years after succeeding to his father's title in 1648, Fairfax resigned as lord general of the army rather than invade Scotland against Charles II. But he mobilised the Yorkshire militia when Scotland invaded England. He then determined to make peace with Charles II, and retired after going to the Hague officially to invite him to assume the crown. He quarrelled with Cromwell before his death, but he was incensed when Charles II desecrated the Lord Protector's remains.

In retirement, Fairfax benevolently held the lordship of the Isle of Man for eight years. He died at Nun Appleton near York, recognised as a man of integrity, liberal principles and a patron of learning. Some said he was too good for his times.

St John Fisher

1469-1535

One of Europe's leading theologians who, with Sir Thomas More, defied Henry VIII and died a martyr's death for his principles.

facing page Portrait of John Fisher (oil on paper, *circa* 1527) after Hans Holbein the Younger. John Fisher became Bishop of Rochester in 1503. He opposed Church reform, refused to recognise Henry VIII as head of the Church of England and was beheaded in 1535. He was canonised in 1935. (*Courtesy National Portrait Gallery, London.*)

Erasmus, the Dutch humanist and outstanding scholar of the Renaissance, said John Fisher was 'the one man at this time who is incomparable for uprightness of life, for learning and for greatness of soul'. That greatness of soul, not to mention his raw courage in his devotion to the Pope and the Roman Catholic Church, led him to defy the will of Henry VIII and to his execution on Tower Hill.

John Fisher was the son of a well-to-do Beverley mercer (dealer in textiles). After his father's death his mother sent him at seventeen to Cambridge, where he developed as a preacher, writer and administrator. He was successively proctor, vice-chancellor and then chancellor for life of his university to which he brought Erasmus to lecture in Greek. As confessor to Lady Margaret Beaufort, mother of Henry VII, he was largely responsible for persuading her to found Christ's and St John's Colleges at Cambridge. In 1504 he became both chancellor of Cambridge and bishop of Rochester, where for thirty years he was a truly pastoral incumbent. In fact, he went by the byname of John of Rochester.

Fisher and Sir Thomas More, chancellor of England, initially came together in the 1520s to combat Lutheran heresy. Both wrote extensively in the cause — Fisher in Latin and More in English for the common reader — and Fisher's book *Confutatio* circulated widely on the continent as a theologian's book for theologians. He strongly opposed any state interference in Church affairs and argued that the Church should reform itself.

Then came Henry VIII's fateful quest for the annulment of his marriage to Catherine of Aragon. Catherine originally married Henry's elder brother,

Arthur, but maintained the marriage was never consummated in the six months before he died. A papal dispensation allowed Henry to marry his brother's widow, only for the king, lacking a male heir, later to argue it had no validity. Cardinal Wolsey sought Fisher's opinion as a holy man of great learning. Fisher concluded that the papal dispensation was valid and remained immoveable on the point, even though he knew Henry regarded opposition to his will as treason. He published his defence of Catherine and preached on her behalf.

Reign of King Henry VIII, an engraving by an unknown artist: Thomas Cromwell, Earl of Essex, Thomas Cranmer, John Fisher, Pope Clement VII, King Henry VIII, Pope Leo X. *(Courtesy National Portrait Gallery, London.)*

Capital punishments decreed by King Henry VIII against Roman Catholics in 1535 are carried out. A (centre): John Fisher, Bishop of Rochester, is beheaded at the age of eighty on the 22nd June. B (left): Chancellor Thomas More is beheaded for high treason on 9th July. C (right): the Countess of Salisbury is beheaded in place of her son who has left the country. A facsimile of a copperplate engraving published in Antwerp in 1587. *(Photo by Hulton Archive/Getty Images.)*

He was clearly a marked man. He was sent to the Tower with More when both refused to take an oath accepting the Act of Succession 1534 because it declared the papal dispensation invalid. They were willing to accept the succession as a proper matter for Parliament, but could not accept the rest of the act because it repudiated papal authority. Fisher suffered relentless persecution during his fourteen months in prison, even though at sixty-five he was suffering from a wasting disease. His fate was sealed a year later when the Pope made him a cardinal.

By then, refusal to recognise Henry as the supreme head of the Church of England had become treasonable. Both Fisher and More managed to withhold that recognition by excusing themselves of an opinion. But Fisher was tricked by the Solicitor-General into declaring confidentially that 'the King was not, nor could be, by the law of God, supreme head of the Church of England'. Those words were treacherously used against him. He was beheaded as a traitor in June 1535 and his head displayed on London Bridge for a fortnight, until it was thrown into the Thames to make way for Sir Thomas More's. Both were beatified in 1886 and canonised in 1935. They share the same feast day — the 9th July.

Guy Fawkes

1570-1606

A unique Yorkshiremen whose part in a Roman Catholic plot to blow up Parliament is spectacularly and joyfully celebrated every 5th November.

No other Yorkshireman is burned in effigy the length and breadth of England and in some former colonies, too. No other Yorkshireman lightens our darkest autumn with a 'reight good do' for children of all ages who love a bonfire and the traditional sweetmeat — Yorkshire parkin — to go with it. And no other Yorkshireman's name comes as readily to the lips as Guy Fawkes' does when children shout 'Remember, remember, the Fifth of November' in raising money for charity — or fireworks.

Indeed, you could argue that no Yorkshireman has done as much for community spirit because of the enormous effort in town and village that goes into celebrating the discovery of his intention to blow up the Palace of Westminster while King James I and his ministers met within. This year the bonfires and bangs will surely be bigger and better than ever, for it is exactly 400 years since his twenty barrels of gunpowder, hidden beneath coal and faggots, were discovered in a cellar under Parliament.

Of course, today Fawkes would be called a terrorist or a freedom fighter, depending on your point of view. He and his fellow conspirators wanted to detonate a big bomb under Parliament in reprisal for increased suppression of Roman Catholics in England. But the centuries have so hallowed his memory — and reduced the standing of politicians — that he is now described as the only man who ever entered Parliament with good intentions.

His fame is remarkable because he was not the originator of the rather naïve and, as it turned out, entirely counter-productive conspiracy to bring about a Catholic uprising, but rather the fall guy in it.

CONCILIVM SEPTEM NOBILIVM ANGLORVM CONIVRANTIVM IN NECEM IACOBI · I ·

MAGNÆ BRITANNIÆ REGIS TOTIVSQ · ANGLICI CONVOCATI PARLEMENTI ·

Bates
Robert Winter
Christopher Wright
Iohn Wright
Thomas Percy
Guido Fawkes
Robert Catesby
Thomas Winter

Vides Spectator humanissime, hic expressas effigies septem Anglorum qui Regem suum eum praecipues Status Anglici Proceribus ad Parlementum, ut vocant conuocatis pulvere tormentario simul horrendo modo in ipsa domo Parlementi euertere voluerunt. Cuius Coniurationis nefandæ Auctores fuere inprimis Robertus Catesby, & Thomas Perci qui sibi deinde adiunxere alios, Videlicet, Thomam & Robertum Winter, Gudonem Fawkens, Johannem & Christopherium Wright quibus demum accessit Bates Roberti Catesbi Famulus. Sed coniuratione hac Diuina providentia & clementia decem antuus horis ante futurã Cessionem Parlamenti Detecta. & Coniuratis persecutis ex iis Robertus Catesbi & Thomas Perci ictu sclopeti periere & eorum Capita domu Parlementi imperpetuant rei memoriam imposita cæteri, cum multis aliis, qui eandem in rem conspirarunt adhuc captui detinentur, dignam facinore sententiam expectantes.

Icy se voient les effigies des sept Seigneurs Anglois lesquels de façon nouuelle et fort Horrible on attente contre le Roy et son estat ainsi entre pins & mines et quantité de puldre de faire Saillir sa Maiesté auec les premiers Du Royaulme et principaux officiers estans en parlement à Westminster les premiers auteurs de la diste conspiration Sont, Robert Catesby et Thomas Percy, ausquels depuis adioinct Thomas et Robert Winter Guido Fawkes Iean et Christophe Wright, et depuis encor le Seruiteur dudit Catesby appelle Bates Mais estante ladist Conspiration decouuerte & lagrac. et providence de Dieu, enuiron dix heures deuant lassemble et assiette dudist parlement et les distes Conspirateurs poursuiuis lesdis premirs auteurs Catesby et Percy sont esté attaincts et tués de Harquebusade leurs testes coupées et portees a Westminster et posees la maison du parlement en memore de l'acte detes Fable Restans auec plusieurs aultes trouues Coulpables dudist faict sont encor prisonniers attendans larrest du Parlement condigne a leurs merites.

The Gunpowder Plot Conspirators.
Guy Fawkes is third from the right.
(Courtesy National Portrait Gallery, London.)

Fawkes was born in York of a good family and went to St Peter's School with two other conspirators, John and Christopher Wright. His spirit of adventure and religious zeal — he was a Catholic convert — led him to enlist in 1593 in the Spanish army, then holding down the Netherlands. By all accounts he was a tall, powerfully built chap with a mass of reddish-brown hair and beard — nothing like the weasly-looking stereotype.

In 1603 he went on a mission to Spain to persuade Philip III to invade England — not surprisingly without success after the fate of the Armada in 1588. A year later Robert Catesby, the plot's leader, wanting a military man not readily recognisable in London, recruited Fawkes without apparently telling him the precise details of the conspiracy.

By now there were so many plotters that security was compromised. A Baron Monteagle got some sort of written tip-off on the 26th October and joined in the Lord Chamberlain's search of Parliament on the 4th November. They found coals and faggots but no explosives. The king ordered another search, and at midnight they uncovered the gunpowder barrels. Fawkes was caught red-handed with a watch, slow matches and touchwood on him. He was tortured on the king's orders and four days later named his fellow plotters. He was hanged, drawn and quartered outside Parliament — the last of the four conspirators left alive to go to the scaffold on the 31st January 1606.

St Peter's School does not, of course, burn Guy Fawkes in effigy. It is not in the habit of burning its old boys.

facing page A Bonfire Night firework display at Hebden Bridge, Calderdale. *(Photo by Andrew Rapacz.)*

above left Guy Fawkes is arrested and brought before King James I; from an original painting by Sir John Gilbert. *(Hulton Archive/Getty Images.)*

above right Guy Fawkes' sheet-iron lantern, given to the University of Oxford by Robert Heywood, son of a justice of the peace who had been present at the arrest of Fawkes in the cellars of Parliament House when the 'Gunpowder Plot' was foiled on the 5th November 1605. *(Ashmolean Museum, University of Oxford/www.bridgeman.co.uk)*

Thomas Chippendale
1718-79

Precious little is known about Thomas Chippendale's early life in Otley, where his memory is celebrated with a statue and an annual dinner to mark his baptism there. He was the only child of John Chippendale, a carpenter, and his wife, Mary, daughter of an Otley stonemason. Mary died young, and John remarried and had seven more children. It is presumed that Thomas received an elementary education at Otley Grammar School and served a family apprenticeship. He is also thought to have worked for Richard Wood, a York cabinetmaker, who later became a Chippendale customer.

We next hear of Chippendale marrying a London woman from St Martin's-in-the-Fields in Mayfair in 1748. She bore him nine children. A year later he rented a house in Long Acre on the fringe of London's then fashionable furniture-making district, before moving to more respectable premises just off the Strand, next to the Earl of Northumberland's mansion.

Then comes the turning point in Chippendale's fortunes — 1754. After moving to St Martin's Lane, where he lived and worked for the rest of his life, he demonstrated his entrepreneurial and marketing flair by advertising his wares. He had the temerity to publish his celebrated *Gentleman and Cabinet Maker's Director* (1754), the most important collection of furniture designs produced up to then in England, illustrating almost every type of mid-eighteenth century furniture. It ran to three editions and contained some 200 plates by way of illustration. He dedicated it to the Earl of Northumberland. His competitors, still relying on word of mouth, thought this terribly *infra dig* but still bought the *Director*, no doubt for ideas.

facing page A detail of the lion's-head carving on Chippendale's library table at Nostell Priory, which is also pictured overleaf. *(Courtesy National Trust Photographic Library/Andreas von Einsiedel.)*

left The library at Nostell Priory, with Chippendale's bookcases, library steps and library table, on which is the painting *Sir Rowland and Lady Winn in the Library* (1767-8) by Hugh Douglas Hamilton, showing how the room has remained largely unchanged in over 200 years. It was Sir Rowland Winn who in 1766 commissioned Chippendale to furnish his country seat after he had inherited it a year earlier. Chippendale was forty-eight, and his reputation as the country's leading furniture-maker was already established following the publication of his groundbreaking book *The Gentleman and Cabinet Maker's Director* twelve years earlier. *(Courtesy National Trust Photographic Library/Andreas von Einsiedel.)*

above A letter dated the 5th November 1767 to Sir Rowland Winn regarding his commission to furnish Nostell Priory, from his 'most obedient humble servant' Thomas Chippendale. *(Courtesy the National Trust, Nostell Priory.)*

And there's the rub. It is in the *Director* that lies much of the speculation and complication about Chippendale furniture. Were all the designs his, or how much had he collated from the work of others at a time when craftsmanship was at its height? His three principal styles — Gothic, Rococo and Chinese — were already established by then, though Chippendale skilfully interpreted them. Whatever the truth, the *Director* was very successful in drumming up orders from the high, mighty and royal, and furniture based on his styles was copied all over Europe and in the Colonies, notably in America.

All this resulted in the term 'Chippendale' being applied indiscriminately to eighteenth-century furniture as a whole. Invoices are the surest guide to authentic Chippendale work. These make Harewood House supreme. Appropriately, you may think, since it is near Otley, it houses the finest collection of Chippendale furniture in Britain, and the bills reveal Chippendale's close collaboration with the designer, Robert Adam, at Harewood and elsewhere. Other important Yorkshire collections are at Nostell Priory, Burton Constable, Newby Hall and with Otley's own Chippendale Society.

Chippendale was not just a furniture man. He was willing to design and supply wallpaper, and offer such services as complete house furnishing, repairs, funerals, removals, furniture hiring and compiling inventories and, most expensively, the supply of mirror glass. After the death in 1766 of his partner James Rannie, a Scottish merchant, he struggled to keep out of the debtor's prison but eventually found financial stability in partnership with Rannie's bookkeeper, Thomas Haig. Chippendale died of tuberculosis and his son, also Thomas, a distinguished cabinetmaker and designer in his own right, carried on the business.

Chippendale maintained his links with his birthplace. A 1770 deed records him helping a relative with the conveyancing of an Otley property.

above left The gentry's fascination in the mid- to late eighteenth century for Chinoiserie-Oriental designs, often in gilt and lacquer, is exemplified by this Chippendale cabinet at Harewood House. (*Courtesy Harewood House Trust.*)

above right Harewood House has many fine examples of Chippendale's work, including the famous Diana and Minerva commode, so called because of the inlaid mythological figures on either side of the coved door. It was commissioned by Edwin Lascelles in 1773 at a cost of £68. (*Courtesy Harewood House Trust.*)

facing page The State Bed at Harewood House was delivered in November 1773 at a cost of £250, plus £150 for the mattresses and linen which was made by the upholsterers in Chippendale's workshop in St Martin's Lane, London. This magnificent bed of intricately carved and gilded wood was only intended to be used by the most important guests, and was barely slept in before it was dismantled in the mid-nineteenth century. It has recently been restored to its full glory, and is now on show at Harewood House for the first time in over 150 years. (*Courtesy Harewood House Trust.*)

Percy Shaw

1890-1976

The eccentric mechanic who became a lifesaver the world over by inventing Catseyes for our roads.

Sir Isaac Newton, we are told, discovered gravity when an apple fell on his head. Percy Shaw certainly demonstrated the inspirational consequences of shock when he invented Catseyes, that simple device which for nearly seventy years has saved untold numbers of lives and limbs on the world's roads.

It was a devil of a job driving home in the pea-soupers they used to experience when Yorkshire was powered and heated by coal, and Shaw's native Halifax, with its forest of mill chimneys, was called the Devil's Cauldron. Shaw used to follow the reflection of his headlights in the tramlines. Then, in an impenetrable fog, he came face to face with the green eyes of a cat on a fence standing between his car and a cliff edge. The penny dropped instantly. Motoring was never to be the same again.

From the age of two, Shaw, one of fifteen children, and his parents lived in the near-derelict remains of Boothtown Mansion, built in 1769. The rent: two shillings and sixpence a week, one eighth of his father's labourer's wages. It was to be the bachelor Shaw's home for life from rags to riches. He was no scholar, but a born mechanic. As he moved from job to job as wireworker, boilermaker, welder, precision engineer and then in business laying garden paths and access roads, he built up a reputation as a gifted engineer. He invented a motor hand-roller to improve his asphalting.

Then came his lucky encounter with the cat and his immediate recognition of the road safety potential of reflected light. He went abroad for the first time in 1930 to Czechoslovakia in search of the right reflecting glass, and found it. Then came a seemingly insuperable problem: how to set the reflecting glass in

Percy Shaw, the man who invented Catseyes, *circa* 1968. *(Photo by Marilyn Stafford/The Observer/ Getty Images.)*

a mould which, as the law required, did not stick out above the surface of the road. He solved it with vulcanised rubber in a metal case.

The asphalter tested his invention under the guise of emergency but entirely unofficial roadworks in Halifax and Bradford, and is reputed to have had the assistance of the police in managing the disruption. These trials revealed the need for self-cleaning reflectors, so he incorporated a squeegee. After five years' research and development he registered his Catseye trade-

mark in 1934 and formed his own company, Reflecting Roadstuds. And high-way engineers took not a blind bit of notice, not even after a fog-bound demonstration on a moorland road.

He easily won an Oxfordshire trial alongside competing studs but the Ministry of Transport was adamant: they were illegal. Ten years after his quest began, the authorities capitulated in 1938 to 'Percy-veerance', as he wryly put it. Come the blackout of the Second World War and Shaw was really in business. The government asked him to produce enough Catseyes to line 1,000 miles of road every month. In spite of rubber-supply problems, Britain was substantially Catseyed, to coin a term, by the end of the war.

Peace brought worldwide demand for his reflecting roadstuds. He built his factory around his home — and even around his beloved sycamore — and the chairman and managing director was often to be found working in his 'muck' in his workshop. His sole luxury, for all his wealth, was a Rolls-Royce Phantom. I shall never forget a colleague, fresh from interviewing this shy but impish eccentric, saying 'There he was, in a sparsely furnished room, sur-rounded by seventeen TV sets — all of them on'.

above Percy Shaw supervising the production of the component parts for reflecting roadstuds, or Catseyes, at his factory in Boothtown, Halifax, in September 1958. *(Photo by Peter Laurie/BIPs/Getty Images.)*

facing page Closeup of a Catseye on a Yorkshire road. *(Photo by Simon Miles.)*

Harry Brearley

1871-1948

The steelworks' cellar boy-made-good whose experiments produced stainless steel and revolutionised the cutlery industry.

If you doubt the impetus the arms trade gives to scientific discovery, think of Harry Brearley. His work immediately before the First World War on the wearing away of rifle barrels led him to discover stainless steel — a boon to the world and not least to its cutlery capital, his native Sheffield.

Brearley was not born a boffin. Far from it. He came into this world in Ramsdens Yard, Wicker, the son of a steel smelter. He followed his father at the age of twelve into Firth's crucible steelworks as a cellar boy, but was quickly moved into the firm's laboratories as a general assistant. He must have been a clever lad with 'inventor' written all over him. By the age of twenty he was a laboratory apprentice, studying at night school and privately at home. He became an expert in the analysis of the properties of steel and established a reputation for solving metallurgical problems.

In 1901 he started a new laboratory for Kayser Ellison before returning to Firths to spend three years managing their Riga, Latvia, plant. He was brought back to Sheffield in 1907 to set up laboratories being established jointly by Firth and another leading Sheffield steel firm, Brown, to conduct research into steelmaking for its own sake. It paid off handsomely.

In 1912 Brearley was asked to investigate why the internal diameter of rifle barrels was wearing away altogether too quickly under the effect of heat and discharge gases. Searching for a tougher steel, he experimented with chromium steels because they had a higher melting point. Lighter chromium steels were by then being used in valves for aero-engines, though the chromium content was only about five per cent.

Workers at a Sheffield steel factory matching pairs of scissor blades in November 1959. The scissors have to cut smoothly along the whole length of the blade, so it is a skilled job. *(Photo by Chris Ware/Keystone Features/ Getty Images.)*

Brearley tried a number of melts with different furnaces, differing chromium contents ranging from six to fifteen per cent and with differing proportions of carbon. While the search was for an erosion-resistant steel, the melting of the first truly stainless steel is precisely dated: the 13th August 1913. It contained 12.8% chromium and 0.24% carbon.

Two men work at an electron microscope being used for research in steel metallurgy at Brown Firth's research laboratory in 1945. Harry Brearley had been instrumental in setting up the laboratory in 1907. (*Popperfoto.*)

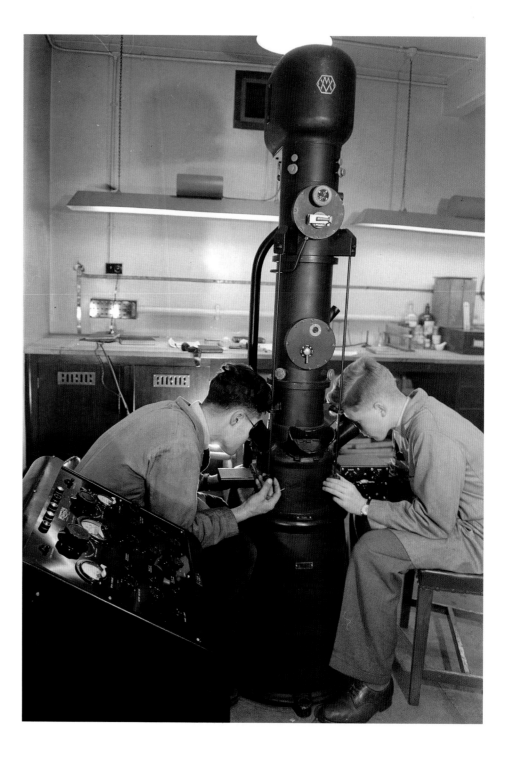

Tests showed it stayed shiny while ordinary carbon steel rusted. When Brearley tried to examine the chromium steel's grain structure by etching it with nitric acid, he found it also resisted chemical attack. It was similarly resistant to food acids such as vinegar and lemon juice. And then the penny dropped: his steel could revolutionise the cutlery industry. Up to then, cutting knives of carbon steel had to be thoroughly washed and dried to prevent rusting, but even then rust stains appeared, as I found with some of my grandparents' cutlery.

It was one thing for Brearley to have developed 'rustless steel', as he originally called it; it was another matter to persuade his conservative steelmasters to use it for cutlery. So he had knives made of it by a local cutler who christened it 'stainless steel'. It was not an instant success. Manufacturers found it difficult to work and customers claimed it did not cut as well as carbon steel. They even called Brearley 'the inventor of knives that won't cut' until the problem was sorted out after the Second World War.

Like all sound Yorkshiremen, Brearley had a well-developed sense of fair play, and resigned from Firths in 1915 over the ownership rights to his invention. He reckoned he was entitled to at least half, employee though he may have been. He walked into a job as works manager for Brown Bayley, Sheffield, where he became a director. He was awarded the Iron and Steel Institute's Bessemer Gold Medal in 1920.

J Arthur Rank

1888-1972

Two Ranks — father and son, both runts of the litter — would qualify for a place among Yorkshire's greatest. But the son, J Arthur — the J was for Joseph — miller, Methodist, film magnate and mega-philanthropist, wins pride of place. He was the 'the man behind the gong' prefacing the best of British films in the cinema's postwar boom.

His father Joseph, born, like his son, in Hull into a successful flour-milling family, was rejected as 'good for nowt' by his father and second wife. He was put to work on the most menial mill tasks, and then incredibly swapped for the son of an Aberdeen miller who got the better of the bargain. Joseph's father even disinherited him on his death in 1874, and a year later his uncles kicked him out of the family business at the age of twenty-one with a mere £500 compensation.

This fired him with a fierce determination to succeed. He built a business, starting with a borrowed windmill, that made him one of the richest men in Britain when he died in 1943. The stock in his flour mills left each of his three sons and four daughters millionaires in their own right. Their family life had been dominated by their father's simple Methodist faith and sharp but honest business brain. They had a happy, privileged but strict Victorian religious upbringing.

J Arthur, the youngest son, was regarded as the 'dunce', likely to get on only in the mill where he was set to learn milling from the bottom up. He inherited his father's teetotalism, tremendous capacity for hard work and his commitment to Methodism. He was a lifelong Sunday school teacher and president of the National Sunday School Union in 1929.

Scottish ballerina Moira Shearer stars in the classic 1948 film *The Red Shoes*, based on the Hans Christian Anderson fairytale of the girl whose shoes wouldn't stop dancing, and directed in Technicolour by Michael Powell and Emeric Pressburger for Rank. *(Photo by Baron/Getty Images.)*

By the time he was forty he had everything — wealth, a family settled in Reigate, Surrey, and social standing — but no personal achievement. He was apparently a dull dog with no aesthetic or cultural interests — just golf, shooting, dogs and cards. Perhaps he was bored. He then hit upon the idea of using film to spread the gospel and later to raise moral standards. It was the start of something stupendous, as film publicists would put it.

Scottish ballerina Moira Shearer stars in the classic 1948 film *The Red Shoes*, based on the Hans Christian Anderson fairytale of the girl whose shoes wouldn't stop dancing, and directed in Technicolour by Michael Powell and Emeric Pressburger for Rank. *(Photo by Baron/Getty Images.)*

Pinewood Studios, built on the orders of film mogul J Arthur Rank in the 1930s and once the choice of directors such as Francois Truffaut and Charlie Chaplin, as well as the home of the James Bond series and the film *Alien*. *(HO/AFP/Getty Images.)*

His development of the religious film-making and distribution industry led him to take over more or less the entire British film industry, from the manufacture of camera lenses through the Pinewood and Denham studios to Odeon and Gaumont-British cinemas. He even took on Hollywood. This earned him many detractors who questioned his motives and integrity. He undoubtedly made many bad films but he did give the British movie industry its golden years with, for example, *Henry V*, *The Red Shoes*, *Oliver Twist*, *Great Expectations*, *Hamlet*, *Blithe Spirit* and *Brief Encounter*.

By 1965, when he assumed control of Rank flour milling on the death of a brother, he was a film magnate, chairman of twenty-three companies and a director of sixty-five. Some dunce! But by then, TV was emptying cinemas that became bingo halls, to the distress of his Church. He diversified into Xerox printing and acquired Hovis McDougall. By his death at eighty-three he had probably given away £100 million to charity, much of it to the Methodist cause.

He was a complex mix of the old-fashioned, naïve, simple believer, the reactionary, the innovator and the shrewd, workaholic tycoon. He communed daily with God and God literally made him an international figure.

Emily Brontë
1818-48

The most graceful, intelligent, tough-minded, home-loving and imaginative of the Rev Patrick Brontë's brood of literary geniuses.

right The dining room at Haworth Parsonage (now the Brontë Parsonage Museum), where the Brontë sisters used to spend their time writing. The couch on the right is the one on which Emily died from consumption on the 19th December 1848, aged only thirty. *(Courtesy of the Brontë Society.)*

facing page *The Brontë Sisters* (oil on canvas, *circa* 1834) by Patrick Branwell Brontë. The figures are, from left to right, Anne, Emily and Charlotte. Emily's poems were included in a pseudonymous publication of 1846, with those of her two sisters; she is widely acknowledged to be the most considerable poet of the three. Her 1847 novel *Wuthering Heights* was not acclaimed as one of the masterpieces of English literature until after her death. *(Courtesy National Portrait Gallery, London.)*

No, I do not have a fixation on *Wuthering Heights*, though my favourite walk from Hebden Bridge is up to the ruins of Top Withens that is supposed to have inspired that remote and forbidding fictional farmstead. There are very good reasons for making Emily the greatest of the Brontës.

148

Emily's writing desk (right) on which she created her masterpieces in verse and prose; and (above) a handwritten poem with marginal sketches. *(Courtesy of the Brontë Society.)*

Of course, the line of least resistance would be to plump for bossy-boots Charlotte. She was the family's literary engine and in *Jane Eyre* wrote one of the greatest novels of the English language, not to mention *Shirley* and *Vilette*. Even Anne, the submissive youngest sister closest to Emily, wrote two distinguished and unconventional novels, *Agnes Grey* and *The Tenant of Wildfell Hall*. Poor Emily could manage only one, though the Brontës' superb biographer, Juliet Barker, thinks Charlotte may have destroyed her second to preserve her reputation.

Of all the four surviving Brontë children, including Branwell — all born in Thornton, Bradford — Emily was the least exposed to the world. Before she was dragged off to Brussels at the age of twenty-four by Charlotte for a year's education and teaching, she had not survived six months away from home without becoming ill. She was home- and self-educated, the most domesticated of them all, and apparently only too happy to remain running Haworth parsonage as long as she could escape into Gondal, the imaginary world chronicled from childhood with Anne. She had an astounding imagination, even in a house of extraordinary talent.

Emily, 'a darling child', was also the tallest and most graceful of the sisters. She was incredibly tough-minded, whether in cauterising herself after being bitten by a dog thought to be rabid, in her unsociableness — she was far kinder to animals than humans — or in her wish to remain known to the world only as Ellis Bell. Bell was the pseudonym under which all three sisters — Charlotte as Currer, and Anne as Acton — originally published their work.

It was the discovery of Emily's poems that fired Charlotte with the ambition to publish them with her own and Anne's, and led them on to literary fame. Charlotte wrote: 'I know no woman that ever lived ever wrote such poetry before'. Emily's teachers rated her more intelligent than Charlotte. M Heger, their Brussels tutor with whom Charlotte fell in love, said Emily had 'a head for logic and a capability for argument unusual in a man and rare indeed in a woman', though somewhat impaired by her 'stubborn tenacity of will'. He added: 'She should have been a man — a great navigator. Her powerful reason would have deduced new spheres of discovery from the knowledge of the old and her strong imperious will would never have been daunted by opposition or difficulty.' He thought her imaginative powers would have been seen to advantage in writing history.

Instead, she wrote *Wuthering Heights*, a story of frustrated passion and cold, driven retribution that earned her, not least of all the sisters, a reputation for dabbling in the 'coarse and loathsome'. Imagine 'little petted Em', tucked away for most of her short life in Haworth, writing this. You can't without appreciating the towering imagination she developed on paper from childhood. Keeper, her dog, followed her to her consumptive grave and then howled outside her room for days. I like to think he mourned not just her kindness and companionship but also the incredible genius he had come to sense in her.

A drawing of her dog Keeper by Emily Brontë. *(Courtesy of the Brontë Society.)*

William Congreve

1670-1729

The greatest English Restoration dramatist who shaped the English comedy of manners through his comic dialogue.

England's nearest approach to Molière — and certainly the greatest English master of Restoration comedy — was born in Bardsey, near Leeds. William Congreve was the son of a soldier who, almost immediately after his birth, was posted to command the Youghal garrison in Ireland. He was educated at Kilkenny, Ireland's Eton, and Trinity College, Dublin, where he shared the same tutor as the satirist, Jonathan Swift, his lifelong friend.

At the age of twenty-one he became a decidedly unserious law student at the Middle Temple. Within a year he had published a near-parody of fashionable romance under the pseudonym of Cleophil, and rapidly entered the company of men of letters as a protégé of John Dryden, who dominated the literary scene.

In 1693 he was an overnight celebrity with his play, *The Old Bachelour*, written, it is said, to amuse himself during convalescence. Dryden said that he had never read such a brilliant first play. His second, *The Double Dealer*, though judged to be far better crafted, was rather a flop. But within two years he had bounced back with *Love for Love*, almost repeating the tremendous success of his first play. He promised to provide the new theatre at Lincoln's Inn Fields, which staged it, with a new play every year. It was a promise unfulfilled, though he did allow it to present his tragedy *The Mourning Bride*, which surprisingly became his most popular play.

Lincoln's Inn Fields had to wait until 1700 for his eventual masterpiece, *The Way of the World*. This may now be his most frequently revived play but it failed with the eighteenth-century audience. And that, so far as drama was

William Congreve (oil on canvas, 1779) by Sir Godfrey Kneller. *(Courtesy National Portrait Gallery, London.)*

The cast of the Sadlers Wells 1934 production of the William Congreve Restoration comedy *Love for Love* wave from the stage in their period costumes. The Huddersfield-born actor James Mason is on the far right. *(Image by Hulton Archive/Getty Images.)*

concerned, was that — and he was only thirty. His massive reputation rests on three of his five plays. They are distinguished by their wit and elegance of dialogue, and their mannered exploration of social values, marital practices, and intrigue and deceit in high places. He rose above other Restoration dramatists in their aim to 'cure excess' in an extravagant era with a delicacy of feeling and language, but he still fell foul of the conservative middle classes who thought writers such as himself and Dryden profane.

He dabbled in verse, wrote librettos for two operas and translated Molière, but was perhaps too comfortably off to persevere with drama. How many dramatic delights, I wonder, were denied us by his relaxed approach to life cushioned by a private income, royalties and a number of Civil Service sinecures?

For his last thirty years he lived on his reputation among such literati as Swift, John Gay who wrote *The Beggar's Opera*, and Alexander Pope and Sir Richard Steele, both of whom dedicated works to him. His affection for Mrs

Anne Bracegirdle, who acted most of his female leads, was well known, but he left her only £200. Instead, the bulk of his estate went to the second Duchess of Marlborough. Congreve was widely thought to be the father of her second daughter, Lady Mary Godolphin, later Duchess of Leeds.

He died from an injury received when his carriage overturned *en route* to Bath and was buried in Westminster Abbey, having apparently been unaffected by the fame which came to him in life. Ten years earlier he had been described as 'being so far from puff'd up with Vanity … that he abounds with Humility and good Nature'.

Bardsey village, the birthplace of the Restoration dramatist William Congreve in 1670. *(Photo by Simon Miles.)*

J B Priestley
1894-1984

A most prolific journalist, essayist, novelist, playwright and controversialist who raised Britain's morale with his wartime broadcasts.

facing page A portrait of John Boynton ('J B') Priestley (oil on canvas, 1970) by Michael Noakes. Priestley had made his name by the early 1930s with *The Good Companions* (1929) and *Angel Pavement* (1930). His first West End play, *Dangerous Corner*, was staged in 1932 and followed by numerous successes including *Time and the Conways* (1937), *The Linden Tree* (1948) and *An Inspector Calls* (1947), this last still proving hugely popular today in Stephen Daldry's touring production. During the Second World War, Priestley's radio *Postscripts* on Sunday evenings made him an international figure. *(Courtesy National Portrait Gallery, London.)*

One of the greatest ironies about J B Priestley is that he was haunted by his experiences of the First World War, yet became as well known for a time as Winston Churchill in the Second World War for his patriotic broadcasts. John Braine, the author, believed that Priestley died in August 1914 somewhere on the Western Front, but that 'a writer was born and what all those millions and millions of words were really for was so that he wouldn't remember the 1914-18 war'.

Jack, as he was known, was the son of a gifted Baptist/socialist headmaster living initially in the German quarter of Bradford. His mother died when he was two and he was brought up by a loving stepmother. Sporty but no scholar, he won a scholarship at thirteen to Belle Vue High School, leaving without qualifications to become a lackadaisical office boy in the wool trade.

From the age of sixteen he wanted to be a writer and prepared himself for the part by acquiring the B after J — B for Boynton — writing poetry and short stories, wearing colourful 'lah-di-dah' clothes and becoming stage-struck at Bradford's Empire and Theatre Royal. His breakthrough came with an imaginary interview with a ragtime singer for which the editor of the *London Opinion* paid him a guinea. In 1913 the *Bradford Pioneer*, the local Labour Party weekly, made him unpaid theatre, book and music critic.

At nineteen he left his office job on the outbreak of war to enlist in the Duke of Wellington's Regiment in Halifax. He emerged from his amazing survival in the Flanders trenches in 1919 to write a series about walking in the Yorkshire Dales for the old *Yorkshire Observer* at a guinea a time. Then he went to Trinity Hall, Cambridge, on an ex-officers' grant to read history and

J B PRIESTLEY

political science. Eight days after graduating, he married the first of his three dark and attractive wives — Pat Tempest, of Bradford. After a year as a postgraduate and with a baby on the way and £50 in cash, he gambled on a career as a writer in London.

This prodigiously fast writer, banging away on an old typewriter, slaved as a reviewer, essayist and reader for a publisher to pay the bills and get himself established. In the process his wife died of cancer, leaving him with two small daughters. He quickly remarried and wrote *The Good Companions*, a novel adapted for stage and screen that made him an international best seller.

Over sixty intensively lived professional years he wrote about 120 books and 50 plays, some of them experimental, especially on the theme of time. They included such well-known works as *Laburnum Grove, Time and the Conways, When we are Married* and *An Inspector Calls*. In 1934, well-heeled and with two mansions to his name, he wrote *English Journey* in which he spoke up powerfully for the poor caught up in the squalor of the 1930s. In the dark days of Dunkirk he attracted up to a third of the BBC's audience after the nine o'clock news with his uplifting *Postscripts* — part of his vast wartime broadcast output that also went to the USA and the Empire.

J B Priestley rehearses one of his *Postscript* speeches for a BBC broadcast to wartime Britain in September 1940. *(Photo by Gerti Deutsch/Picture Post/Getty Images.)*

above   A pen-and-ink portrait of J B Priestley *circa* 1973 by fellow Bradford-born artist David Hockney. *(Bradford Art Galleries & Museums, UK; www.bridgeman.co.uk.* © *David Hockney.)*

left   Priestley's ashes are buried in the churchyard at Hubberholme, upper Wharfedale. *(Photo by Simon Miles.)*

Always loosely on the Left, he helped to form the Campaign for Nuclear Disarmament. He accepted the Order of Merit after turning down a knighthood and a peerage, and also received the freedom of the City of Bradford. The tiny church at Hubberholme in upper Wharfedale records the scattering of his ashes there in 'one of the smallest and pleasantest places in the world', as he put it.

Alan Bennett

1934-

Satirist, dramatist, author, actor and social commentator whose wit and ability to make the most mundane lives fascinating has delighted the nation for more than forty years.

right The *Beyond the Fringe* comedy team during filming for the BBC in August 1964: (left to right) Alan Bennett, Peter Cook, Dudley Moore and Jonathan Miller. *(Photo by David Newell Smith/The Observer/Getty Images.)*

facing page A portrait of Alan Bennett by Tom Wood dating from 1993. Like the sitter, the artist is from Yorkshire — his studio is at Dean Clough, Halifax — and is known for his somewhat mysterious, idiosyncratic symbolism. The objects in the portrait — the plug and the paper bag — deliberately provoke questions without providing answers. *(Courtesy National Portrait Gallery, London.)*

He once confessed he might have become a vicar 'because he looked like one'. He added: 'This is not as silly as it sounds. People often end up doing what the mirror tells them what they are suited for, while feeling themselves quite different inside. And in the process, whole lifetimes are thrown away'.

Alan Bennett was saved, if that is the right term, from the Church by that essentially anti-Establishment activity — satire. He appeared at the Edinburgh Festival in 1960 with Dudley Moore, Peter Cooke and Jonathan Miller

ALAN BENNETT

Tinted postcard of Armley Library, at the junction of Stock Hill and Wesley Road. This imposing building was the favoured reading place for the young Alan Bennett. He recalled it later as a 'grand turn-of-the-century building with a marble staircase'. *(Courtesy Leeds Library & Information Services.)*

in a satirical review *Beyond the Fringe* that he co-wrote. They went on to play to tremendous acclaim in London and New York. His three compatriots later blazed their various ways across stage and screen, while Bennett steadily established himself as the nation's most observant dramatist, with an acute ear for dialogue and a wondrous ability to release an embarrassment of emotions from the most mundane of suburban lives. His latest triumph came in 2004 on his seventieth birthday with *The History Boys*, a semi-autobiographical return to his Yorkshire roots set in a grammar school of twenty years ago.

History will surely recognise him as a witty, devastatingly accurate and emotive social commentator on the infinite gradations of the English class system and the human condition in the second half of the twentieth century. It is clear from his work that, from a very early age, he was observing and storing away impressions of life in Armley, Leeds, where he was born, the son of a Co-op butcher who played the violin. Like most of us brought up in the West Riding during the war, we learned that 'life is generally something that happens elsewhere', as he put it. I recall that the mere mention of Hebden Bridge on the wireless was a week-long wonder. By the age of five, he records, he knew 'he belonged to a family that without being in the least bit remarkable or eccentric...managed never to be quite like other families'. Thank goodness.

After Upper Armley National and Leeds Modern Boys' School, he went up to Exeter College, Oxford, on a scholarship to read history. He got a first, became a don and ironically found release from his chronic shyness in acting. Within three years he and his colleagues were reducing Edinburgh to 'near hysteria'. The potential vicar became celebrated for his sermon, eventually entitled *Take a Pew*, in which he tries vainly to be 'with it'.

He escaped, though not completely, from clerical roles and character acting into writing for radio, the stage, TV and the cinema. From his pen came such memorable works as *Forty Years On*, *The Old Country*, *An Englishman Abroad*, *A Private Function*, *The Madness of King George*, *The Lady in the Van*, based on a woman who lived in a van in his street, and a bestselling book *Writing Home*, a collection of prose writings and reminiscences. His *Talking Heads* character-driven monologues for TV in the late 1980s were masterpieces. He also endeared himself to millions with his wonderful adaptation of *Wind in the Willows*.

Bennett, the intensely private, bachelor intellectual with appropriately firm views about the world, for years kept close to his people with a home at Clapham in the Dales, to which his parents retired. He is still president of Settle Civic Society.

Alan Bennett as Graham in 'A Chip in the Sugar' from his acclaimed *Talking Heads* series. *(Copyright © BBC.)*

Charles Laughton

1899-1962

An actor of memorable originality and power who left enduring images of Henry VIII, Captain Bligh, Nero and Quasimodo.

He was no oil painting. He thought his great moon face and tubby body ugly. He was an early hippy — and off-white with it. He never took to soap and water. One catty actor at the Royal Academy of Dramatic Art said he hadn't 'a hope in hell of ever working, looking the way he does'. And he turned out to be difficult — really difficult — to direct. But, boy, could Charles Laughton act. And how he worked at it with prodigious energy. His biographer, Simon Callow, claims that half a dozen of his performances in the 1930s set him apart from almost any other actor of the century for their originality and intensity.

He left the world with enduring images of Henry VIII, one hand grasping a flagon and the other tossing joints of devoured venison over his shoulder, Captain Bligh, Rembrandt, Nero and, not least, Quasimodo in *The Hunchback of Notre Dame*, where his grotesqueness disturbed us and moved us to tears. His range of characterisations was amazing across thirty-seven plays and fifty-two films. And yet this Scarborough lad came late to his profession.

He was born in his parents' Victoria Hotel, Scarborough, in the full flush of its phase as a Victorian spa. They took over the Pavilion Hotel when he was thirteen and, on his return from Stonyhurst, where he did not distinguish himself, he was set to learn hotel keeping from the bottom up — if London's Claridges can be described as such — by his ambitious Catholic mother, Eliza. After two happy years there, he returned to Scarborough to sign up as a private with the Royal Huntingdonshire Rifles with the First World War still a year to run. He froze, starved and fought in the trenches, and was gassed a week before the armistice. He suffered the consequences for the rest of his life.

Charles Laughton on the set of the 1958 film *Witness for the Prosececution* directed by Billy Wilder. In 1955 Laughton had made a sole, and successful, foray into directing, with *The Night of the Hunter*, but his later career consisted chiefly of giving readings, and making radio and television appearances. Self-doubt assailed him and he once said 'I have a face like the behind of an elephant'. *(Rex Features.)*

Anthony Wysard's 1936 cartoon 'Jointly and Severally' pays tribute to Laughton's profusion of roles banking up behind Henry VIII, Rembrandt and Captain Bligh. In 1936 he became the first British actor to appear at the Comédie Française, playing Sganarelle (in French) in Molière's *Le Médecin malgré lui*. The Parisian audience gave him a standing ovation. *(Courtesy National Portrait Gallery, London.)*

It was six months before he overcame his black war-induced depression to assume hotel command since his father was ill. He gave the Pavilion a facelift while he made his mark with the Scarborough Players, notably as Willie Mossop in *Hobson's Choice*. And then at twenty-four, after a long performance managing the Pavilion, he chucked it all in for a nine-month course at RADA. His brother Tom took over the hotel. He collected the Bancroft gold medal from Sybil Thorndike, and George Bernard Shaw predicted a brilliant career for him within a year. And within that year this genius, starting at the top, played seven featured roles in seven new West End productions. He also married the outrageous, elfin actress Elsa Lanchester — a union that was to survive his bisexuality.

After West End stardom, he went to Broadway and then, with intermittent forays back to the UK, settled in Hollywood where he became an American citizen. He worked with Komisarjevsky, De Mille, Korda, Hitchcock, David Lean and Billy Wilder, and the brightest of Hollywood stars, collaborated with Brecht and Losey on the first production of *Galileo*, directed his only feature film, the brilliant *Night of the Hunter*, and toured America giving readings and teaching. He once said that 'great acting is like painting … not imitation — that is merely caricature and any fool can be a mimic! … The better — the truer — the creation, the more it will resemble a great painter's immortal work'. Laughton was a great artist.

Andrew Marvell

1621-78

The MP whose political reputation overshadowed his poetry for 200 years until the twentieth century recognised him as one of the best lyrical poets.

Andrew Marvell was a man of many parts: scholar, linguist, traveller, tutor, MP and spy. But it took a long time before his poetry was appreciated. T S Eliot bestowed the highest praise on him. Marvell, he said, spoke 'more clearly and unequivocally with the voice of his literary age than Milton'. More than 200 years after his death, he came to be seen as one of the best secular metaphysical poets.

This Holderness man was never easy to pin down. He guided his friend, the blind poet John Milton — to whom Eliot referred — in Cromwell's funeral procession, yet later sat in the Restoration Parliament. He wrote a superb poem ostensibly in praise of the Lord Protector, yet it is remembered for its compassion towards the executed Charles I. He numbered among his friends the leading revolutionary Puritans, yet some of his Restoration pamphlets were noted approvingly by Charles II. He loved solitude, yet he was a public man, and a diligent and effective MP for Hull from 1659 to his death. He was a love poet who never married and was capable of coarse satire as well as ethereal verse.

Some would say he was a Vicar of Bray. Others would argue he was his own man. Eliot claimed he was a 'lukewarm partisan'. He is frankly a bit of a mystery. In his day, he was known as a satirist and pamphleteer, champion of political liberty and an incorruptible patriot.

None of his poetry survives in his own hand and none of his best-known poems was published in his lifetime. His reputation as a poet was largely formed in the twentieth century, though his 'witty delicacy' captivated Charles

A portrait of Andrew Marvell (oil on canvas, *circa* 1665-60) by an unknown artist. *An Horatian Ode upon Cromwell's Return from Ireland* (1650) is regarded as Marvell's greatest political poem, but he is best known for works such as *To his Coy Mistress* and *The Garden*. After the Restoration he turned to writing bitter satires. *(Courtesy National Portrait Gallery, London.)*

Andrew Marvell visiting his friend John Milton (oil on canvas) by the Victorian artist George Henry Boughton. *(Private Collection, Bonhams, London, UK/www.bridgeman.co.uk.)*

Lamb and Tennyson is reputed to have walked up and down declaiming Marvell's lines:

> 'But at my back I always hear
>   Time's winged chariot hurrying near.'

Marvell was born the son of the vicar of St Germain's at Winestead-in-Holderness just before his father became assistant preacher at Holy Trinity, Hull. He was educated at Hull Grammar School, and was in the last of his seven years at Cambridge when his father drowned crossing the Humber. His demise may have ended his son's academic career.

As civil war engulfed England, Marvell spent five years abroad, apparently as a tutor. He was certainly tutor to the daughter of another Yorkshire great, General Sir Thomas Fairfax at Nun Appleton, between York and Selby, where from 1651-2 he wrote his notable poems *Upon Appleton House* and *The Garden*. From 1653 he was tutor to Cromwell's ward before, in 1657, becoming

The politician Lord Danby (seated left) offers a bribe of 1,000 guineas to the poet and Member of Parliament Andrew Marvell, circa 1660. 'Marvell spoke little in the House of Commons; but his heart and vote were always in the right place ... King Charles, having met him once in private, was so delighted with his wit and agreeable manners, that he thought him worth trying to bribe. He sent Lord Danby to offer him a mark of his majesty's consideration. Marvell, who was seated in a dingy room up several flights of stairs, declined the proffer, and, it is said, called his servant to witness that he had dined for three successive days on the same shoulder of mutton, and was not likely, therefore, to care for or need a bribe.' From *Specimens with Memoirs of the Less-Known British Poets* (1864) by the Rev George Gilfillan. *(Photo by Hulton Archive/ Getty Images.)*

assistant to Milton as Latin secretary in the Foreign Office. Two years later he became a Hull MP.

The evidence suggests that he was far from being a natural supporter of Cromwell, but his poetry shows a growing admiration for him during the 1650s. Yet his *An Horatian Ode Upon Cromwell's Return from Ireland* includes this tribute to Charles I:

'He nothing common did or mean
Upon that Memorable Scene:
But with his keener Eye
The Axes edge did try.'

He also penned his memorable respects to Cromwell on his death:

'I saw him dead, a leaden slumber lyes,
And mortal sleep over those wakeful eyes.'

He then became part of the Parliamentary opposition to Charles II but did not challenge his kingship, though he turned to satire and pamphleteering. He was hardly a toady, but he was a survivor. He was his own man and had a delicious pen.

Ted Hughes
1930-98

Britain's greatest and most controversial poet of the twentieth century 'who looked nature in the eye with all her magic and all her cruelty'.

They have described his work as animalistic, anti-human and nihilistic. Others see Edward James Hughes, the late Poet Laureate, in a different light — as a continuation of the Celtic bardic tradition, as a modern shaman.

He was born the son of a carpenter in the deeper recesses of what was the last Celtic kingdom of England — Elmet in the West Riding. He lived in Mytholmroyd, near Halifax, for only the first seven years of his life before his family moved to Mexborough. But in those formative years he absorbed the

A class photo at Burnley Road School, Mytholmroyd, in 1937. 'Teddy' Hughes is fifth from the left on the top row. *(Courtesy Peter Speak & Donald Crossley.)*

Poet and author Ted Hughes in 1993. Hughes was born in Mytholmroyd in 1930; when aged seven, he and his family moved to Mexborough, where his father ran a paper shop. He later won a scholarship to Pembroke College, Cambridge. His best-known works include his first verse collection *The Hawk in the Rain* (1957), *Crow* (1970) in collaboration with the American artist Leonard Baskin, the prizewinning translation *Tales from Ovid* (1997), and numerous children's writings including the short story collection *How the Whale Became* (1963) and the novel *The Iron Man* (1968) which was later turned into an animated film. Hughes was married to the American writer Sylvia Plath from 1956 to 1963, when she committed suicide. Their relationship inspired his last, and arguably greatest, collection of poems, *Birthday Letters*, published in 1998. (*TopFoto.co.uk/UPPA Ltd.*)

above 1 Aspinall Street, Mytholmroyd, the birthplace of Ted Hughes and where he spent his early years. *(Courtesy Peter Speak & Donald Crossley.)*

above right The Pennine village of Mytholmroyd in 1950: (from the left) the Co-op, Aspinall Street with Ted's birthplace on the end of the terrace, Mount Zion Methodist Chapel, and the bridge over the Rochdale Canal. Of the four mentioned, only 1 Aspinall Street remains. *(Courtesy Peter Speak & Donald Crossley.)*

essence of Elmet's harsh Pennine environment and, hunting with his elder brother, its nature red in tooth and claw. It remained a dominating influence over his writing that runs the full gamut of the bardic range, transmitting language (dialect), history, wisdom, myth, mysticism and the occult.

As a friend, Dr Caroline Tisdall, put it at his memorial service in Westminster Abbey: 'He looked nature in the eye with all her magic and all her cruelty'. Seamus Heaney, the Nobel Prize winner, saw him as 'a guardian spirit of the land and language'.

It was from a millstone grit terrace house in Aspinall Street, Mytholmroyd, that Dr Tisdall's 'voice of the countryside' became an observer of the natural world and continued its study in the unlikely surroundings of Mexborough where, as a grammar school boy, he made friends with a gamekeeper's son.

After National Service in the RAF he read English at Cambridge, but later changed to archaeology and anthropology. There he met and married Sylvia Plath, an unstable American poet, who encouraged him to enter his manuscript *The Hawk in the Rain* for a Poetry Center competition. This established him as a leading poet of his generation. After two years teaching in America, they returned in 1959 to the UK to full-time writing. Four years later Plath gassed herself, leaving him with two young children. Seven years on, lightning struck a second time — Assia Wevill, the woman for whom he had left his wife, similarly took her life with that of their daughter. Hughes became a hate figure for feminists, who repeatedly removed his name from Plath's tombstone in Heptonstall churchyard. Just before his death, Hughes broke his long silence on this personal tragedy by publishing his acclaimed *Birthday Letters*, a book chronicling his tragic love story and separation from Plath.

After the savage experience of his middle years, Hughes retreated into privacy and writing with a new wife in Devon. He was a prolific poet who also wrote prose, opera librettos, stage plays and children's books. He succeeded John Betjeman to become Yorkshire's third Poet Laureate in 1984. Twelve days before his death, the queen conferred on him the Order of Merit. He had just won the Whitbread Award for *Tales of Ovid*, a reworking of Ovid's *Metamorphoses*.

Hughes is honoured with his name carved on a rock on remotest Dartmoor. A boyhood friend, Donald Crossley, also perpetuates his memory with conducted tours around my native valley to places that inspired Hughes's poetry, notably in *Remains of Elmet*. For me, the true bard reveals himself in this bleak poem that gives the book its title:

'Death struggle of the glacier
Enlarged the long gullet of Calder
Down which its corpse vanished.
Farms came, stony masticators
Of generations that ate each other
To nothing inside them.
The sunk mill-towns were cemeteries
Digesting utterly
All with whom they swelled.
Now, coil behind coil,
A wind parched ache,
An absence, famished and staring,
Admits tourists
To pick among crumbling, loose molars
And empty sockets.'

Yorkshire's two other Poets Laureate were: Rev Laurence Eusden, of Spofforth, from 1718 to 1730; and Alfred Austin, of Leeds, from 1896 to 1913.

David Hockney

1937-

The most publicised and popular British artist since the Second World War, distinguished for his wit, versatility and range.

above Portrait of My Father (oil on canvas, 1955). *(Private Collection. © David Hockney; www.bridgeman.co.uk.)*

facing page David Hockney *circa* 1965. *(Observer/Getty Images.)*

He decided he wanted to be an artist when he was eleven. He was so determined that, as a scholarship boy at Bradford Grammar School, he relegated himself to the bottom form so that he could study art. He drew for the school magazine and produced posters for the debating society as a substitute for homework. At the age of fourteen, the rebel wanted to go to the junior Bradford School of Art but the authorities would not let him leave grammar school until he had completed his general education. He left for art school at the very first opportunity — when he was sixteen after his GCEs. He says he spent twelve hours a day there for four years.

That was the making of David Hockney, painter, draughtsman, printmaker, photographer, stage designer, the most publicised British artist since the Second World War and an immensely successful experimenter in the ways of pursuing his chosen profession. He was for a time perhaps the world's most prolific artist by fax. One memorable event in 1989 at Salts Mill, which houses the largest collection of his works in the world, was built around the faxing of his art.

Hockney — the fourth of four brothers and a sister — is a natural talent. His family was not artistic, though his father had a slight interest in art and his eldest brother had wanted to be an artist, too. One of the first oil paintings he sold was *Portrait of My Father*, painted on Saturday afternoons after the subject had finished work. It brought the magnificent sum of £10 in 1954 at a Yorkshire artists' exhibition in Leeds.

Hockney marked time for two years from 1957-9. As a conscientious objector, he worked in hospitals in Bradford and Hastings in lieu of National

Salts Mill, Saltaire, Yorks (oil on two canvases, 48" x 120" overall, 1997) by David Hockney. (© David Hockney.)

Service. He did little work but read Proust. He emerged from three brilliant years at the Royal College of Art with a gold medal in the graduate competition. He recognised two groups on arrival — the traditionalists who carried on as they had done in art school, and the adventurous involved in the art of their time. There are no prizes for guessing which the ebullient Hockney identified with. His early work, when he was coming to terms with his homosexuality and searching for a style, earned him a reputation as a leading Pop artist, though he rejects the label.

Between 1961-3 he discovered the freedom of America in New York (where he bleached his hair) and Los Angeles, and visited Italy and Berlin. He made such rapid progress that he was financially independent soon after leaving the Royal College and never needed to teach to make a living. By 1966 he had had five one-man exhibitions in Europe. Living in Paris in the early1970s, he produced a series of etchings in memory of his hero, Picasso.

Much of his work is autobiographical, including portraits and self-portraits, and scenes with friends, and still life. It is distinguished by flair, wit and versatility, and brilliant draughtsmanship. His popularity was reflected in the success of a Tate retrospective in 1988. It attracted 170,000 visitors, worthy of an Old Master. He is noted for his designs for the stage, including costumes and sets, notably for Glyndebourne and the Metropolitan Opera in New York. He has lived permanently in Los Angeles since 1978, where he has a studio in the Hollywood Hills. But he maintains his connections with Yorkshire, and the Saltaire galleries demonstrate his affection for his native heath as well as his brilliance.

facing page *Model with unfinished self-portrait* (oil on canvas, 1977). (*Private collection. © David Hockney; www.bridgeman.co.uk.*)

above left David Hockney on the beach outside his American home. Hockney has lived permanently in the United States since the late 1980s. (*Photo Paul Harris/Getty Images.*)

above David Hockney at the 2004 Royal Academy Summer Exhibition, where he also exhibited. Hockney is sitting in front of *Reverse* by Jenny Saville. The exhibition is the largest open contemporary art show in the world, showing a wide range of new work by both established and unknown living artists. (*Photograph by James Veysey, Camera Press London.*)

Henry Moore

1898-1986

The twentieth century's greatest sculptor, whose work became 'the acceptable face of modernism'.

Henry Moore in 1909 aged eleven, the only surviving picture of him as a child. *(Reproduced by permission of the Henry Moore Foundation.)*

Henry Moore reminds me of Freddie Trueman. If one's ambition was to be 't' best bloody fast bowler in t' world', the other was determined to become 't' best bloody sculptor in t' universe'. They both made it — and not merely in their own estimation.

Part of Moore's charm was that he seemed so normal and modest in the light of the abnormality and some would say pretension of his work. Yet he numbered himself among the greatest in the history of art.

Henry Spencer Moore had a lot going for him from birth, even if he was the seventh of eight children of a Wheldale Colliery miner living in a two-storey brick terrace house in Castleford. His father, Raymond, had escaped the penury of farm work in Lincolnshire for the pit and was no ordinary miner. He had read Shakespeare, taught himself to play the violin, and learned enough mathematics and engineering to become a pit deputy. He was also extremely ambitious for his brood, most of whom became teachers. Henry adored his mother, Mary, the inspiration, perhaps, for the femininity and motherhood that came to dominate his sculpture.

He had the early good fortune to become fascinated with Michaelangelo, thanks to a Sunday school teacher. This early interest in sculpture was developed by school visits to churches, where he was struck by the caricatured heads on corbels, and by carving wooden tipcats for the childhood game. And then Alice Gostick arrived as Castleford Secondary School's art teacher to bring out his artistic talent. More than fifty years later she bequeathed her house to her pupil.

Like several others in this book, Moore survived gassing — his at the Battle of Cambrai in the First World War — to spend two hard-working years at Leeds School of Art before graduating in 1921 with, among others, Barbara Hepworth, to the Royal College of Art in London. He remained a true York-shireman, even though he spent the rest of his life, married to an upper-class

Henry Moore in his studio at Hoglands, Hertfordshire, in January 1983. It was his home for more than forty years, and is currently being restored by the Henry Moore Foundation. *(Copyright © popperfoto.com.)*

Henry Moore's *Reclining Figure: Arch Leg* (1969-70), at the Yorkshire Sculpture Park near Wakefield. *(Photo by Helen Pheby, reproduced by permission of the Yorkshire Sculpture Park and the Henry Moore Foundation.)*

Russian girl, in London, Kent and, from 1940, in Hertfordshire. He did not, for example, overpay his assistants even though they enabled him to proliferate his work, by carving and casting editions of his works, which in turn helped to endow the Henry Moore Foundation with £40 million capital to support the fine arts. It's an ill wind.

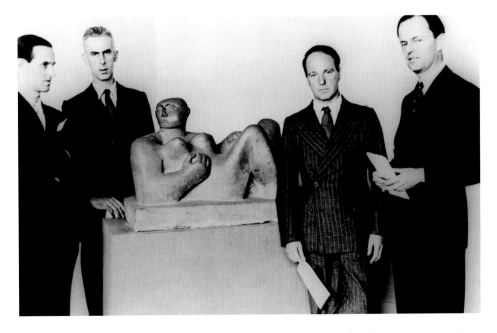

The proliferation tended to undermine Moore's quality in later years, but by then his reputation as the twentieth century's greatest sculptor was secure. His drawings were widely acclaimed, notably as a war artist of miners down Castleford's pits and people using the London Underground as an air-raid shelter. Yorkshire's influence can, perhaps, be found in the solidity as well as the holes and tunnels of his carvings. He also drew inspiration from the artefacts of Mexico, Africa and Oceania, and from ancient Greece and Renaissance Italy, and made mother and child, reclining Earth mother, and foetus and womb his main themes.

His genius was to transmute his preoccupations through stone, bronze and wood into what his biographer, Roger Berthoud, describes as 'the acceptable face of modernism'. His modernism came in for a lot of stick but, curiously, the more stick he got, the more commercial he became. It became almost *de rigueur* for great corporations, public bodies and connoisseurs to have a Henry Moore; *Knife Edge Two Piece*, for example, forms the backdrop for many political TV interviews outside Parliament. He had many powerful advocates and the British Council promoted his work abroad as a cultural asset. He is honoured in his own county, notably at the Yorkshire Sculpture Park at Bretton Hall near Wakefield.

above left   Henry Moore (centre right) with Graham Sutherland (left) and John Piper at the time of their joint exhibition at Temple Newsam near Leeds in 1941. The exhibition was opened by Kenneth Clark (right), at the time the director of the National Gallery in London, and a powerful and continuing advocate of Moore's artistic genius. *(Reproduced by permission of the Henry Moore Foundation.)*

above   Moore's *King and Queen* of 1952-3 is the most famous of all his bronzes, and the anthology piece which collectors and museums most ardently seek. This example (the fourth casting) became the best known, and is situated on a rocky outcrop overlooking Glenkiln Loch on Sir William Keswick's Scottish estate. The queen was modelled on Moore's wife Irena. *(Photo by Errol Jackson. Reproduced by permission of the Henry Moore Foundation.)*

Frederick Delius

1862-1934

The rebel who rejected wool for music to become one of the most significant figures in the revival of English music.

facing page Frederick Delius, the Bradford-born composer of choral and orchestral works, by Ernest Procter (oil on millboard, 1929). Delius's success was established in Germany before his merits were recognised in Britain, largely due to Sir Thomas Beecham. Works such as the opera *A Village Romeo and Juliet* (1907) and *A Mass of Life* (1909) have increased in stature over the years, and ironically pieces such as *Brigg Fair* are now seen as quintessentially English. *(Courtesy National Portrait Gallery, London.)*

They don't come much more fascinating than Frederick Delius. If his father could have denied him his musical ambition, he would have done so. He went on to be regarded as the equal of Elgar in originality, if not in range or invention, and become one of the most significant figures in the revival of English music at the end of the nineteenth century. Yet he was of German stock and spent little of his adult life in England.

He was born Fritz (later anglicised to Frederick) Theodor Albert, the fourth of fourteen children of Julius, a Bradford wool merchant from Germany. His father admired and encouraged his precocious musical talent on piano and violin. But he demanded absolute obedience, and expected Frederick to apply himself to the family business after Bradford Grammar School and the International College at Isleworth in London. Fortunately, Frederick was a rebel who found wool an absolute bore. Eventually, his father bowed to the idea of his starting an orange-growing business in Florida with the son of a Bradford dyer.

Oranges no more inspired Delius than wool. When his partner fell ill, he went to Jacksonville, twenty miles from the orange groves, in search of a doctor. While a neighbour looked after the sick man, he lingered in town for a week, playing the piano in a music shop and taking lessons in orchestration from a New York organist who had heard him playing. He then found a job as a music teacher in Virginia, before his father capitulated and let him go to Leipzig to study music properly.

Delius had the luck to be befriended by Edvard Grieg, Norway's national composer, who not only encouraged him to become a composer but charmed

above left Frederick Delius at the turn of the nineteenth century, aged about thirty. *(From* Delius: A Life in Pictures *by Lionel Carley and Robert Threlfall, and reproduced with permission.)*

above right A card party at Leipzig: (left to right) Nina Grieg, Edvard Grieg, Johan Halvorson, Delius and Christian Sinding. *(From* Delius: A Life in Pictures *by Lionel Carley and Robert Threlfall, and reproduced with permission.)*

Julius into agreeing that his son's exceptional talent should be rewarded with an allowance. In 1888 Delius embarked on his chosen career in Paris and drew inspiration from many sources — English, Norwegian, Danish, German and French literature, North American Indians and negroes, and the contrasting landscapes of Florida and Scandinavia. He married a German painter, Helene Jelka Rosen, in 1903 and they settled in her house at Grez-sur-Loing, near Fontainebleau.

He wrote extensively, from songs and small-scale instrumental and orchestral pieces, to major orchestral and choral works, and six operas. He was in his pomp as a composer from 1900 until the outbreak of the First World War. His opera with a voodoo theme *Koanga* led the Germans to claim him as a national composer. Sir Thomas Beecham became his most enthusiastic protagonist in the UK after hearing his great work, *Appalachia. On hearing the first cuckoo in spring, Summer nights on the river* and 'The Walk to the Paradise Garden' (from his operatic masterpiece *A Village Romeo and Juliet*) earned him a much too narrow reputation as a composer of pastoral miniatures.

By the 1920s he was beset by blindness and increasing paralysis. A young

Scarborough organist, Eric Fenby, later a professor at the Royal Academy of Music, then brought about a late flowering. In 1928 — a year before Delius was made a Companion of Honour — Fenby offered his services to the composer and, after a disastrous start, became his amanuensis. With Jelka's soothing presence, Delius dictated to the patiently dedicated Fenby, and completed his unfinished works and some new ones before his death. Fenby, who died in 1997, brought Delius' coffin to be silently buried at midnight, as directed, in a Limpsfield country churchyard in Surrey.

The Bradford-born composer Frederick Delius, who had become paralysed and blind in 1924, being read to by his wife the artist Jelka Rosen at their home in Grez-sur-Loing, near Fontainebleau, France, on the 15th February 1928. *(Photo by Hulton Archive/Getty Images.)*

John Barry

1933-

The world's most successful film composer with four Oscars, two Academy Awards and thirteen James Bond film scores.

This will have them stumped down at the Mucky Duck's quiz night. What does Yorkshire have in common with the films *Born Free*, *The Lion in Winter*, *Out of Africa*, *Dances with Wolves*, *Midnight Cowboy* and more than a dozen James Bond films? The answer is John Barry. He is not a household name in Yorkshire, though he ought to be because he is the world's most successful film

The original line-up of the John Barry Seven, *circa* 1958: from the left: Mike Cox, Derek Myers, Fred Kirk, Ken Golder, John Barry, Ken Richards, Keith Kelly. *(Courtesy Ken Golder.)*

composer. That, he admits, is what he always wanted to be. His scores for films have won him, among other things, four Oscars (for the first four films listed above) and two Academy Award nominations.

Barry, the youngest of three children, was born John Barry Prendergast in York. He was marinated in film and music from birth. His father owned a chain of cinemas, including the Rialto that served as a concert hall, and his mother was a classically trained pianist. He was educated at the Bar Convent and at St Peter's School, where he formed a film society, and was given a thorough grounding in basic musicianship by his teacher, Dr Francis Jackson, master of music at York Minister, who had led a dance band during the Second World War and was a big band enthusiast.

In February 2005, film composer John Barry was awarded with a BAFTA Fellowship at the British Academy Film Awards for his lifetime's contribution to the film industry. *(Photo by Getty Images.)*

The distinctive James Bond theme was first heard in the 1962 film *Dr No*, starring Sean Connery and Ursula Andress. Though there is some argument about who composed the theme tune, John Barry certainly arranged and orchestrated it for the screen, and went on to compose the music for most of the films in the Bond series. *(Rex Features.)*

Barry served in the Green Howards for nine years, played the trumpet in the regimental band, and took a qualification in composition. While serving, he sent arrangements for popular songs to Ted Heath, Johnny Dankworth and other band leaders, and several were broadcast. In 1957 his father loaned him £5,000 — a tidy sum then — to help him establish with some of his army pals the John Barry Seven, a rock and roll group in which he was vocalist as well as trumpeter. After hearing the band at the Rialto, the impresario Harold Fielding signed them up to appear with Tommy Steele at Blackpool. They appeared weekly on *Six Five Special* and grew in fame because of their association with Paul Anka, Adam Faith and Russ Conway.

Barry was hired to score Adam Faith's movie *Beat Girl*, and the blend of big brass and big guitar anticipated the James Bond music. Within five years of launching his band, he was propelled into film orbit by being hired to help score the first two Bond films, *Dr No* and *From Russia with Love*. There is some controversy over who actually composed the Bond theme for *Dr No*, one of the most recognisable pieces of film music, but what is not in doubt is that

Barry became resident composer and scored thirteen of the seventeen films in the series. Shirley Bassey made the tracks for *Goldfinger*, *Diamonds are Forever* and *Moonraker* international hits, as did Tom Jones with *Thunderball*.

Barry has composed the scores for more than thirty-five films as well as stage musicals and television specials. The *New Musical Express* described his theme for *The Persuaders* as the best TV theme ever written. He is a very private person who has shown an astonishing range of musical influences, and a remarkable ability to establish the mood and place of a film through its score. The workaholic lives in Oyster Bay, New York, with his family, and retains both his accent and affection for his native Yorkshire.

The film composer John Barry at his piano, December 1967. He is perhaps best known for the theme to the James Bond films. *(Photo by Express/ Express/Getty Images.)*

Dame Janet Baker

1933-

A home-grown mezzo-soprano of international fame who blossomed through dedication into an all-rounder — opera, oratorio, Lieder and song — of great presence, expression and clarity.

Dame Janet Baker shows you where hard work, dedication and a voice with a presence can get you when it is anchored in sound Yorkshire common sense. It takes you to the top of your profession in opera, *Lieder*, oratorio, song and as a recording artist.

She was born, the daughter of an engineer, in Hatfield near Doncaster. Her parents were not particularly musical, though her father, a special constable, sang in the York Police Choir during the Second World War. She also had an urge to sing, and her elementary school teacher said she would either be a singer or a writer.

She won a scholarship (for her aptitude in English) to York College School, attached to the Minster, and sang in the annual Minster choir festival. But then her father took a job in Grimsby, where she was unhappy and temporarily silenced. She took advice not to sing for two years as her voice was breaking and her wonderful mezzo-soprano emerged from the high soprano of childhood.

Back in York with her family, she took a job in a bank, studying music in her spare time in Leeds where she joined the Leeds Philharmonic Choir. When her father moved again — to Stockton-on-Tees — she faced a big decision: should she go with her family, or transfer with the bank to London and continue her studies?

She sought the advice of her Leeds Phil conductor, Allan Wicks, who had selected her as a soloist in Haydn's *Nelson Mass*. Should she try to study music seriously? 'Yes, of course', he said, though he seemed immediately to regret his

Dame Janet Baker by Daphne Todd (oil on board, 1987). Mezzo-soprano Dame Janet, one of the leading singers of her time, is equally renowned for opera, oratorio and recital performances. She made her operatic debut in 1956, and from the mid-1960s appeared at Glyndebourne, Covent Garden and with the English National Opera. The part of Kate Julian in Benjamin Britten's *Owen Wingrave* was written for her. *(Courtesy National Portrait Gallery, London.)*

British mezzo-soprano Dame Janet Baker *circa* 1965. *(Photo by Erich Auerbach/Getty Images.)*

reaction. The bank was accommodating, so off Janet went to London. By then — 1953 — she had won the open class for contralto and the silver rose bowl for all voices at the Harrogate Spring Festival.

The soprano soloist, Ilse Wolf, had told her that if she ever went to London she should seek out Helene Isepp as her tutor. After six months working in the bank by day and taking Mrs Isepp's lessons in the evening, she was exhausted, homesick and without money to finance further study. In a family conference, Mrs Isepp told Janet's parents that she should be able to earn her living as a singer but could not say whether she would have the luck or dedication to go further.

She proved her dedication and Mrs Isepp's forbearance over fees — Janet paid her what she could out of her earnings as a part-time college reception-ist and singing with the Ambrosian Singers — and Ilse Wolf's support carried her through. Her first radio broadcast was on the BBC in July 1955 and her first broadcast recital three months later on the Northern Home Service.

Then came the breaks. She was second in the Kathleen Ferrier Prize in 1956. One of the judges, Lord Harwood, since one of her great supporters, later admitted they got it wrong. She made her first operatic appearance in Oxford University Opera Club's performances of Smetana's *The Secret*. And she acquired a husband, Keith Shelley, who became her manager as her career took off.

She is celebrated for her vocal expression, stage presence and projection of words, and her interpretation of Mahler, Elgar, Bach, Handel and Benjamin Britten. Her diary of her last year as an opera singer — 1981-2 — reveals the sheer physical fitness and stamina required of a singer, and her attachment to Yorkshire. The latter is reflected in her long-standing chancellorship of the University of York.

Dame Janet Baker as Maria Stuarda at the English National Opera in 1982. *(Clive Barda/PAL.)*

Sir Leonard Hutton

1916-90

England's first professional cricket captain (who never led Yorkshire), and a commanding opening batsman of elegance, artistry and phenomenal success.

'I was introduced to my father at the age of thirteen'. So said Richard Hutton at the inauguration of the 364 Club at Headingley in August 2003, to mark the sixty-fifth anniversary of the greatest innings by an Englishman in Test match cricket by the opening batsman of my generation. We knew what he meant. Len Hutton was not merely poised, elegant and phenomenally successful at the wicket; he was also dedicated to his profession on the field and off it. If, as John Woodcock wrote, 'he wanted to be judged as a person as much as in his role as a cricketer', he amply achieved his ambition. He commanded lifelong respect and some would say awe.

Just before his death I was able to pay my respects in a curious way. Having heard that neither Hutton nor his England partner, Cyril Washbrook, had been to No 10, I persuaded Margaret Thatcher to invite them to a 'general reception'. Washbrook was shy and seemed overawed. Hutton obviously enjoyed himself with the cast of *Coronation Street* which, he said, he watched regularly on TV.

I never thought, when I just got into Headingley before the gates closed in 1948 to watch Hutton and Washbrook face the might of Lindwall and Miller, that I would once be instrumental in entertaining them. At that time, I was industriously dreaming of and practising to emulate Hutton. Sir Leonard was never a dreamer, but then he didn't need to be. Born of a family whose religion was cricket in Fulneck, the village near Pudsey with a Moravian Protestant community, was a sort of predestination.

He first played for Yorkshire a month short of his eighteenth birthday — he made a duck — and survived the testing experience of performing in a driven

A 1937 photograph of Sir Leonard Hutton. *(Courtesy National Portrait Gallery, London.)*

Len Hutton is congratulated by Bill Brown on scoring 364 and thereby breaking Don Bradman's first-class innings record during the Test match between England and Australia at the Oval, London, in 1938. *(Photo by Central Press/Getty Images.)*

side to become a household name within four years. He was only twenty-two when he scored his 364 at the Oval in the longest innings then played in first-class cricket — thirteen hours and twenty minutes from Saturday morning to Tuesday morning — an epic unrelieved by a single six.

But there you have the clue to Hutton. Alan Ross said he was the 'embodiment of so many classical ideals — discipline, restraint, concentration, correctness and elegance of execution', that he came to be thought of, among other things, as infallible. When he failed, it seemed England would. His

achievement is all the greater for losing two inches off his left arm in a wartime accident. It did not seem to make any difference. In five years before the war he scored 11,658 runs with an average of 48.98. From 1945, when he returned to first-class cricket, to his retirement ten years later he made another 28,292 runs at 58.81.

In his second era, he became England's first professional captain without having led Yorkshire. He regained the Ashes in 1953 and retained them in Australia two years later. But his dual role as batsman and leader — and a very difficult tour of the West Indies in 1954 — drained him so much that he took himself and his bad back off to retirement in Surrey. We were left with memories — as we are now — of a rather battered face, a beautiful stance, unhurried artistry, almost regal command of the crease, a superb cover drive and 129 first-class centuries (nineteen of them in Tests), or a century very nearly every six innings. And, just fancy, this reserved, taciturn Yorkshireman with the occasional twinkle in his eye did it all without a helmet or an unseemly flourish.

F S Trueman

1931-

Freddie Trueman in 1949, the year of his first-class debut for Yorkshire. *(Photo by Express/Express/Getty Images.)*

I have two favourite cartoons. One by Jak is of a battered, dishevelled President Giscard d'Estaing arriving home late from a summit with Margaret Thatcher to be greeted by Mme d'Estaing with the words: 'I thought I told you to stay away from that woman'. The other is Roy Ullyett's caricature of Freddie Trueman on the point of delivery, breathing fire from his nostrils, shedding perspiring beads of molten lead, with fanged teeth, asbestos boots, and charred stumps and scorched earth in his wake.

For all their exaggeration, both cartoons speak the truth. Thatcher, Trueman's political heroine, took no prisoners in argument and Freddie none in cricket. He was purpose-built for a fast bowler with a powerful and relatively compact frame, a magnificent, defining action and with aggression to match. He was also the answer to England's prayers after their postwar battering by the Australians, Lindwall and Miller.

Freddie's slightly bow-legged swagger, his black forelock across his forehead, his malevolent purpose, his ability to catch fire and incinerate the opposition, and his repartee, sublime and profane, real or imagined, not to mention his impulsive nature, made him a 'reight character'. His performances over twenty years made him an international legend. As he told the Australian batsman Norman O'Neill, who thought two Indians at the next table were talking about him: 'Aye, they talk about me all over t' world, Norm, lad'. As, indeed, they did.

His performances testify to his amazing stamina and consistency. His England bowling average was 21.57 with a strike rate of 49.53. His first-class

Yorkshire and England cricketer F S 'Freddie' Trueman at the Grosvenor House Hotel, London, in February 2001, on the occasion of his seventieth birthday and the Fiery Fred Collection Auction where a lifetime of cricketing memorabilia was sold off. *(Ian Walton/ Allsport.)*

record and one-day records were 18.29 and 43.27 and 18.10 and 35.2 respectively. His achievement is perhaps all the greater for the very serious groin injury he received as a young teenager, batting without protective box, which put him out of the game for two years. For the average lad, that would have been it; but not Freddie. As John Arlott put it, he was one 'who knew from the first moment he considered such matters that he was going to be a great fast bowler'.

From his miner's terrace house at Scotch Springs next to a pit heap near Stainton, South Yorkshire, he was nurtured through Maltby Modern School, and the Roche Abbey and Sheffield United clubs to Yorkshire winter coaching classes under Bill Bowes. He made his first-class debut with Brian Close and Frank Lowson at Cambridge University in May 1949. He was fast but erratic and profligate. He then endured for virtually two seasons what passed for Yorkshire's man-management — neglect.

This was the last thing Freddie needed. He responded to encouragement, as Ronnie Burnet later proved as his Yorkshire captain. Then, uncapped and unproven, he was picked for the Rest v England at a Bradford Park Avenue

Freddie Trueman celebrates with his England team-mates after taking his 300th Test wicket during the fifth Test against Australia at the Oval on the 15th August 1964. (*Allsport Hulton/ Archive.*)

Fred Trueman bowling during the first innings of the Lords Test match against Australia, during the 1961 Ashes series. The batsman behind him is R N Harvey. *(TopFoto.co.uk/PAL.)*

Test trial. He bowled Len Hutton, but Yorkshire still left him languishing. Somehow he survived its indifference as the fast bowling competition melted away and his control improved. He made his case in 1951 when he was capped, and his career took off in 1952.

That was the year when India collapsed at Headingley, with the scoreboard reading unbelievably 0 for 4, three of the wickets down to Freddie. The legend was born. He retired at thirty-seven, having bowled more than 20,000 overs — Herculean labour for a fast bowler — surpassed all in taking 307 Test wickets in only sixty-seven matches, scored some 9,000 runs including three centuries, and made 438 catches, most of them as a predatory short leg. He lived on as a forthright writer, BBC commentator, night-club performer, after-dinner speaker and Yorkshire committee man, and now, most importantly, as a Yorkshire Dalesman. Home is the hunter …

Brian Clough

1935-2004

T' best bloody manager England's
soccer team never had – and
t' best bloody centre forward
England hardly ever used.

They called him 'Old Big 'Ead'. In fact, that was what he called himself. He was as *brussen* as they come, as they say in Hebden Bridge. Brian Clough had much to be brussen about.

He took two unfashionable, second division Midlands soccer clubs — Derby County and Nottingham Forest — to promotion, both in his second season as their manager, and then both to the Football League championship. And at Forest he not only won the European Cup in 1978-9 but retained it the following season. That is more than Sir Alex Ferguson can claim at Manchester United with all his untold riches.

Clough was the best Englishman never to have managed his country's national team, and the best centre forward to have won only two measly England caps. Just imagine scoring 251 goals in 274 games for Middlesbrough and Sunderland, and only twice representing your country. This can only be explained by rank prejudice against an awkward, opinionated and fearlessly forthright Yorkshireman.

Clough was born the cocky fifth of Joseph and Sarah Clough's close and disciplined working-class family of eight children in Valley Road, Middlesbrough. His early ambition was to play cricket for Yorkshire. He was no scholar, though he did become head boy at school, but he knew his way to goal. The story of his life was the difficulty others had in appreciating his soccer talents.

His break into League football at Middlesbrough was delayed by National Service in the RAF. He did not, of course, make the national RAF team. When

Brian Clough in 1979, when he was manager of Nottingham Forest. After an unsuccessful spell at Leeds United, Clough joined Forest in January 1975. Under his astute guidance, the club won promotion from the old second division just two years later, the league title in 1978, the European Cup in 1979 and then went on to retain the trophy the following year. *(Copyright © popperfoto.com.)*

he finally got into the Middlesbrough first team, he scored 197 goals in 213 League games. But for a leaky defence, Middlesbrough would surely have been promoted. Then at Sunderland he bagged fifty-four goals in sixty-one League games, only to have his career effectively ended at twenty-seven by a serious knee injury.

That is how, after coaching at Sunderland, he became the youngest League manager at Hartlepool, where he formed perhaps the most formidable managerial partnership in soccer with Peter Taylor, formerly Middlesbrough's reserve goalkeeper. In less than two years the regular seekers after re-election stood high in the Fourth Division. Taylor provided the counsel, and Clough the leadership and flair.

Then Clough made what he described as the worst mistake of his life. Having built a championship side at Derby, he and Taylor resigned because they felt they were not properly appreciated. They temporised at Brighton and, this time on his own, Clough lasted only forty-four days at Leeds United before player power evicted him.

It was the prelude to something bigger: eighteen trophy-winning years with Nottingham Forest, the last eleven on his own after he fell out with

Taylor. In addition to promotion, the League Championship and the European Cup (twice), he won the League Cup four times (twice losing finalist); European Super Cup (once losing finalist); the Simod Cup; and the Zenith Data Cup. Forest were also twice World Club finalists, once League runners up and Wembley Cup finalists in 1990-1. It all ended in tears in 1993 when Forest were relegated. Clough blamed drink — a demon he conquered as it threatened his life.

He achieved all this as a self-confessed player's manager, running the show, insisting on discipline, fitness and no nonsense on the field — referees used to say he made it easy for them — and by keeping it simple. 'I'm sure the England selectors thought, if they took me on, I'd want to run the show', he said. 'They were shrewd because that's exactly what I would have done.' More's the pity he didn't.

above left Nottingham Forest manager Brian Clough and his assistant Peter Taylor at the European Cup Final in Munich on the 30th May 1979, in which Forest beat Swedish side Malmo 1-0. Brian Clough was one of the most successful managers in British football, and took both Forest and Derby County to the League Championship. *(Copyright © popperfoto.com.)*

above Clough shouts instructions from the dug-out to his Nottingham Forest team as they play his former club Leeds United in September 1979. *(Copyright © popperfoto.com.)*

Alan Hinkes

1954-

The greatest mountaineer that Yorkshire has ever produced — and the first Briton to climb all fourteen of the world's highest mountains.

At around 7pm on the 30th May 2005, Alan Hinkes made history. In driving snow he climbed the last of the world's fourteen peaks that exceed 8,000 metres — and became the first Briton to do so. After dedicating eighteen years of his life to overcoming this tremendous challenge, the fifty-year-old former teacher from Northallerton finally conquered Kangchenjunga (8,587 m), the third-highest peak at the treacherous eastern end of the Himalayas.

left Alan Hinkes in early 2005 as he got ready to conquer his fourteenth and final peak over 8,000 metres — Kangchenjunga in the Himalayas, which he had attempted to climb twice before without success. *(Berghaus.)*

facing page Alan Hinkes climbing in Scotland, in preparation for another difficult ascent in the Himalayas. *(Berghaus.)*

top Alan Hinkes with his daughter Fiona and grandson Jay. *(Berghaus.)*

bottom Alan Hinkes on the summit of Dhaulagiri in 2004 holding a photo of his daughter Fiona and grandson Jay which he takes to the top of every summit. *(Berghaus.)*

It was third time lucky for he had been thwarted twice before on Kangchenjunga: in 2000 when he broke his arm falling into a crevasse; and in 2003 when he contracted a severe bronchial infection on his way to base camp. His physical and mental endurance were tested to the utmost by his successful ascent. Deep fresh snow lay all the way up from base camp with a very high risk of avalanches. He was beaten back by the weather on his first summit attempt on the 29th May, and on the second his Sherpa partner, Pasang Gelu, had to halt fifteen minutes from the top through exhaustion. Hinkes had never experienced worse summit conditions. Fortunately, he located Pasang on his way back from the peak and they made it back to base camp two days later.

'Getting back was one of the best feelings of my life', said Hinkes. 'The final summit push was without a doubt the hardest climb of my life.'

Mountaineering is not in Alan Hinkes' blood. His father was in business as a plumber in Northallerton and his mother a hospital ward sister. It was Northallerton Grammar School that gave him mountain fever. As a boy he loved wandering the North Yorkshire countryside, and then his school's Outdoor Activities Society introduced him to fellwalking in the North York Moors, the Yorkshire Dales and the Lake District. A new economics master took him rock climbing, and by the age of eighteen he had progressed to the Alps.

At Newcastle-upon-Tyne University he qualified as a teacher in outdoor education and geography, became president of his college's mountaineering club, and taught in Hexham and Gateshead, latterly in a school for the handicapped. He became a professional mountaineer by accident. His education authority refused him leave of absence to go on a 1984 Everest expedition so he resigned, intending to become a supply teacher on his return. Instead he turned professional and became a technical consultant with Berghaus, the mountaineering equipment firm. He is also an accomplished photographer, writer and lecturer. He has climbed alone or with parties of up to eight, and latterly with Pasang.

His quest to conquer the world's fourteen highest mountains began in 1987 when he climbed Shisha Pangma (8,046 metres). The rest fell regularly with the spring climbing seasons: 1988, Manaslu (8,163 m); 1990, Cho Oyu (8,201 m); 1991, Broad Peak (8,047 m); 1995, K2 (8,611 m); 1996, Everest (8,848 m, filmed for a Channel 4 TV documentary *Summit Fever*), Gasherbrum I (8,068 m) and Gasherbrum II (8,035 m); 1997, Lhotse (8,516 m); 1998, Nanga Parbat (8,125 m); 1999, Makalu (8,463 m); 2002, Annapurna (8,091 m); and 2004, Dhaulagiri (8,167 m).

On each summit he has photographed himself with a picture of his daughter Fiona, and latterly with one of Fiona and his grandson, Jay. He observed the ritual during his ten minutes on top of Kangchengjunga in spite of the awful conditions.

His climbing philosophy in the extremes of altitude where there are no rescue teams and where helicopters cannot fly has served him well. 'I climb to live, not to die — the summit is always optional but returning is mandatory'. He has returned to world acclaim — and incidentally set a new challenge for fifty-year-old Yorkshiremen: beat that.

Barbara Jane Harrison

1945-1968

An air stewardess whose courage and selfless devotion to duty in staying with a crippled passenger in a blazing plane posthumously won her a George Cross.

Air stewardess Barbara Jane Harrison. *(VC & GC Association.)*

Imagine yourself a stewardess on one of the old Boeing 707 airliners when the number two engine catches fire soon after take off from Heathrow. The engine falls off, leaving a fierce fire burning on the wing. The pilot manages to get the plane back on the ground in two and a half minutes, but the fire intensifies.

Your job at the rear of the aircraft is to open up an escape route from the tail. You and your fellow steward manage to open the rear galley door and inflate the chute, only for it to become twisted. The steward climbs out to straighten it so that the passengers can slide down it to safety. But, once outside the aircraft, he cannot get back in. You are left on your own amid flames and explosions to encourage people to jump out. Soon there is no way out at the back, so you have to direct passengers to another exit. But there is one passenger, an elderly cripple, in one of the seats at the rear, who cannot go anywhere. Your duty requires you to try to save the old and the lame.

Barbara Jane Harrison, the twenty-two year old British Overseas Airways Corporation stewardess, did just that. Her body was found near to that of the disabled passenger.

For her 'courage and selfless devotion to duty', Miss Harrison was posthumously awarded the George Cross. She was one of only five women to be directly awarded the George Cross since its inception in 1940. Three of them — Odette Churchill, Noor Inayat-Khan and Elizabeth Szabo — were special agents in occupied France during the Second World War.

Miss Harrison was born in Bradford, and educated at Scarborough and Doncaster High Schools for Girls, before taking a job in a bank in Doncaster

and later as a nanny in San Francisco. She was an adventurer who loved travel and so became a stewardess. She was buried at Fulford, York, where her heroism is commemorated as well as in Heathrow Airport Chapel.

Other Yorkshire George Cross awards

The George Cross is a civilian award equal to that of the Victoria Cross. So far there have been 152 awards since its introduction by King George VI in 1940. Including Miss Harrison, Yorkshire has at least five of them. They are:

John Dixon, of Bradford, an electrician who, though badly burned and in danger of electrocution, rescued a crane driver from a fire at a Lincoln foundry in 1940.

The burnt-out fuselage of the BOAC Boeing 707 which crash-landed at Heathrow Airport on the 8th April 1968 after one of its engines had caught fire on take-off. The bravery of air stewardess Barbara Jane Harrison in the ensuing cabin fire saved the lives of several passengers. Miss Harrison lost her life in the tragedy, and was posthumously awarded the George Cross in August 1969. *(Photo by Evening Standard/Getty Images.)*

Anthony John Gledhill, of Doncaster, a Metropolitan Police constable who chased a car containing five bandits for five miles in 1967 at speeds of up to 80mph under a hail of fifteen shots before closing with them when the bandits' car crashed.

Graham Leslie Parish, from Sheffield, a sergeant in the RAF Volunteer Reserve, burned to death in 1943 trying to rescue an injured passenger from a transport plane in the Sudan.

Geoffrey Gledhill Turner, from Sheffield, a sub-lieutenant in the Royal Navy Volunteer Reserve who in 1941 miraculously survived defusing a badly damaged mine dropped in the blitz in Liverpool when it exploded.

There are, however, some 400 people deemed to be holders of the George Cross by virtue of their having won the Empire Gallantry Medal, or the Albert or Edward Medals. We know that a Yorkshireman won one, but it could be as many as twenty, sixteen of them miners, since so many of the incidents were in Yorkshire mines. Incomplete records force me to differentiate between certain Yorkshire holders and possibles.

Yorkshire holders

George William Beaman, from Sheffield, a South Kirkby miner for his courage during a rescue in 1936 after two underground explosions. *Possibles:* In the same incident Norman Baster, a colliery agent, and James Pollitt, a miner, also won the George Cross.

Geoffrey Riley of Huddersfield, who was awarded the George Cross in October 1944 when, as a fourteen-year-old schoolboy, he tried to rescue an elderly woman from a flash flood in the Holme Valley. He died in January 2005. (*VC & GC Association.*)

Geoffrey Riley, a fourteen-year-old Huddersfield schoolboy, for his attempt to save a woman trapped by a flood in a cloudburst at Holmfirth in 1944, in which the woman and his father died. Riley, who died early in January 2005, was one of the youngest recipients deemed to have won the George Cross. There is an even younger Yorkshire possible — Harwood Henry Flintoff, who was thirteen when he rescued his farmer-employer from a bull at Farnwell, North Yorkshire, again in 1944.

Other possible Yorkshire holders

Six mineworkers at Bentley Colliery in a firedamp explosion that killed forty-five in 1931: Ernest Allport, Richard Edward Darker, Oliver Soulsby, Frank Sykes, Philip William Yates and Samuel Jarrett Temperley, an assistant surveyor, who all became George Cross holders for their gallantry during the rescue.

Sydney Blackburn, a shotfirer at Barnsley Main Colliery, for rescuing others, regardless of his own safety, after an explosion in 1947.

John Weller Brown, connected with Richmond, for his part in rescuing

A rescue team comes up for a rest between attempts to reach miners trapped in Lofthouse Colliery in March 1973. Seven men died after a coal seam they were working became flooded. Sadly, this was all too often a tragic scene at a coalmine disaster — disasters in which sixteen mineworkers in Yorkshire were awarded the George Cross. *(Photo by The Observer/Getty Images.)*

those killed and injured in an explosion at an ammunition railhead at Catterick Bridge Station in 1944.

Bernard Fisher, a crane driver at Steel, Peach and Tozer, Sheffield, for rescuing in 1939 another gantry crane driver from a fire in his cabin fifty-five feet above the ground.

Fred Haller, a deputy at Rossington Main Colliery, for rescuing a man overcome by gas in an underground heading.

Percy Roberts Havercroft, a miner at Waleswood Colliery, Sheffield, for rescuing, in very dangerous circumstances in 1917, ten men severely injured when their descending cage collided with an ascending one.

George Christopher Heslop, manager of Loftus ironstone mine, for rescuing two men buried under a roof-fall in 1935.

Walter Holroyd Lee, a workman at Wombwell Main Colliery, for rescuing two men trapped under a fall of roof in 1947 after one rescuer had been killed by another fall.

Charles Smith and Matthew Thompson, both miners at Askern Main Colliery, for rescuing a miner trapped under a fall of roof in 1940.

CSM Stanley Elton Hollis VC

1912-72

The Green Howard who won the only VC on D-Day

Stanley Hollis VC sat for a portrait in 1946 wearing battledress, and his gallantry and campaign medals. *(The Green Howards Museum.)*

To represent the forty-six exceptional Yorkshiremen who have won the Victoria Cross in battle, I have chosen one who had the remarkable distinction of winning the only VC on D-Day, the 6th June 1944. He was CSM Hollis, who performed heroically during the 6th Green Howards' assault on Gold Beach in Normandy.

He was the eldest and very strong-willed son of a Loftus fishmonger who later moved to Robin Hood's Bay. At seventeen he joined Rowland and Marwood of Whitby as an apprentice navigating officer, and made regular voyages to West Africa with the Elder Dempster Line until blackwater fever ended his career at sea.

He then worked in North Ormesby as a lorry driver and with a brick company, and married and had two children — a boy and a girl. He carried his rebellious streak into the Territorial Army, where his obstinacy was tolerated long enough for him to be mobilised on the outbreak of the Second World War to help form the 6th Battalion, Green Howards.

He had a long, action-packed war, and matured into one of the finest and bravest NCOs the Green Howards have known. He swam for his life from Dunkirk, served in Iraq, Palestine and Cyprus, and fought his way from El Alamein to Tunis before being wounded in Sicily. His battalion was then posted home to prepare for the liberation of Europe because Montgomery wanted the 50th (Northumbrian) Division to break German resistance in Normandy.

On D-Day, CSM Hollis landed his company exactly as planned after firing a couple of long Bren-gun bursts into a pillbox on the seawall 'to keep German

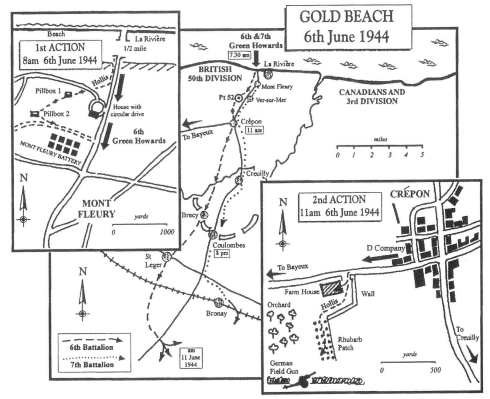

The advance of the Green Howards at Gold Beach on D-Day (main map); and (inset maps) the actions undertaken by CSM Hollis, sergeant major of 'D' company of the 6th Green Howards, for which he received the Victoria Cross, the only one awarded on D-Day. *(The Green Howards Museum.)*

heads down'. Making their way up the beach, he saw a burst of fire from a pillbox into the rear of the leading platoons. Immediately, he charged it alone, firing a Sten-gun from the waist. He put a burst into it through the firing slit and then a grenade. Inside, he found two Germans dead and the rest wounded or dazed. Coming out, he noticed a trench led to another pillbox about 100 yards away. Advancing on it, he saw Germans emerge with their hands up and took fifteen to twenty prisoners.

Later that day, clearing a village, a sniper grazed his cheek as he tried to take out a German field gun which had partly demolished his temporary farmhouse shelter. He then found two of his Bren-gunners trapped in the house. Under fire and in full view of the enemy, he went forward with a Bren-gun to distract attention while his men escaped.

His gallantry on D-Day twice prevented the enemy from holding up the advance and saved the lives of many of his men. He was invested with the Victoria Cross by King George VI. After the war he regularly returned to

CSM Stanley Hollis of the Green Howards clambers on top of the enemy pillbox hindering the Allied advance from Gold Beach to the south of La Rivière, and drops a grenade through the slit. He subsequently destroyed another pillbox nearby and captured over fifteen German prisoners. For this and his bravery in the village of Crépon two hours later, he was awarded the Victoria Cross. *(The Green Howards Museum.)*

France to recount his exploits for young officers from the Staff College studying the invasion — all the more effectively for his sense of humour.

In Civvy Street this extraordinary soldier settled back into family life and, his biographer Mike Morgan says, he was a gentle and loving father. He worked as a sandblaster in a steelworks, a partner in a motor repair business, a ship's engineer and as a publican, including managing the Green Howards in North Ormesby. The Green Howards Regimental Museum at Richmond has his VC and clasp on display.

The Victoria Cross awarded to CSM Hollis is now on display at the Green Howards Museum, Richmond. *(The Green Howards Regimantal Museum.)*

Yorkshire's Roll of Honour

The Victoria Cross, cast in bronze from the cannons captured at Sevastopol in the Crimean War, is the most coveted medal for bravery. A total of 1,352 VCs have been awarded since the medal was introduced in 1856. There are forty-six Yorkshire winners, including CSM Hollis. They are listed below, showing rank at the time, birthplace, regiment and an account of their valour. A star * denotes a posthumous award.

*A/Flt Sgt Arthur Louis Aaron DFM, Leeds, 218 Squadron, RAFVR, for bringing his aircraft home from a raid on Turin in 1943, in spite of terrible injuries.

Capt William Barnsley Allen DSO, MC and bar, Sheffield, RAMC, for tending the wounded under heavy fire after a shell had exploded ammunition in France in 1916, and, though wounded four times himself, continuing until the last man had been treated and removed. He then tended a wounded officer before reporting his own injuries

*Pte Eric Anderson, Fagley, Bradford, 5th Bn, East Yorkshire Regt, for three times rescuing the wounded under heavy fire in Tunisia, 1943; he was rendering first aid to a fourth when mortally wounded.

*Sgt Alfred Atkinson, Leeds, 1st Bn, Yorkshire Regt, mortally wounded going out for the seventh time under heavy fire to get water for the wounded in South Africa in 1900.

*T/2nd Lieut Donald Simpson Bell, Harrogate, 9th Bn, Yorkshire Regt, for attacking and destroying a machine gun under heavy fire across open ground on the Somme in 1916, dying in a similar operation five days later.

Pte William Boynton Butler, Leeds, 17th Bn, West Yorkshire Regt, for picking up an unexploded shell under heavy fire in France in 1917, using himself to shield a party of men until they were out of danger and then throwing the shell over the trench before it exploded.

Sgt Laurence Calvert MM, Hunslet, Leeds, 5th Bn, KOYLI, for capturing single-handedly under heavy fire two machine guns and killing their crews in France, 1918, ensuring the success of an operation.

Pte George William Chafer, Bradford, 1st Bn, East Yorkshire Regt, delivering a message on his own initiative under heavy fire after the messenger had been knocked out by a shell in France in 1916, although severely wounded, and choking and blinded by gas.

Pte Tom Dresser, Pickering, 7th Bn, Yorkshire Regt, for delivering an important message to the front line at a critical period in France, 1917, though twice wounded and in great pain.

*T/Lt Col Bertram Best-Dunkley, York, commanding 2/5th Bn, Lancashire Fusiliers, for leading an assault on enemy positions in Belgium in 1917 under fierce fire until all objectives had been gained and later beating off an attack. Died of his wounds.

*Lt Cdr Eugene Esmonde DSO (and great-nephew of a Crimean VC), 825 Sqdrn, Fleet Air Arm, Thurgoland, for leading a Swordfish attack on three German battleships in the Straits of Dover in 1942, until his plane, which had sustained a direct hit, burst into flames.

Sgt Robert Grant, Harrogate, 1st Bn, 5th Regt (later Northumberland Fusiliers) for carrying to safety under heavy fire in India, in 1857, a private whose leg had been shot away.

*Cpl. John William Harper, Doncaster, 4th Bn, York and Lancaster Regt, for leading his section under heavy fire across 300 yards of exposed ground in Antwerp in 1944; a position was captured largely due to his self-sacrifice.

*T/2nd Lt John Harrison MC, Sculcoates, Hull, 11th (S) Bn, East Yorkshire Regt, for twice leading his company against an enemy trench in France in 1917, and then trying to knock out a machine gun to save the lives of many of his company.

Lt Alan Richard Hill (later Hill-Walker), Northallerton, 2nd Bn, Northamptonshire Regt, for rescuing three men under very heavy fire in South Africa, 1881.

*A/Capt David Philip Hirsch, Leeds, 4th Bn, Yorkshire Regt, for establishing under intense machine-gun fire a defensive flank in France in 1917, and then encouraging and steadying his men under counter-attack, standing on a parapet until he was killed.

Pte Joel Holmes, Halifax, 84th Regt (later York and Lancaster), the first to respond at Lucknow, India, in 1857 to a call for volunteers to work under heavy fire a gun at which all the artillerymen had become casualties.

Pte Matthew Hughes, Bradford, 7th Regt (later Royal Fusiliers), for twice running for ammunition across open ground under heavy fire in the Crimea in 1855, and for bringing in a badly wounded soldier and then an officer from the front.

Pte Charles Hull, Harrogate, 21st Lancers, for rescuing an officer from certain death at the hands of tribesmen on the North West Frontier in 1915, lifting him onto his horse under fire from close range.

*L/Cpl Thomas Norman Jackson, Swinton, 1st Bn, Coldstream Guards, for volunteering to follow his company commander across a canal in France in 1918, to capture a machine-gun post and then leading a charge into an enemy trench.

Pte Arnold Loosemore DCM, Sheffield, 8th Bn, Duke of Wellington's Regt, for crawling through partially cut wire in Belgium in 1917, killing single-handedly twenty enemy, shooting another three with his revolver after losing his Lewis gun, shooting several snipers and bringing back a wounded comrade under heavy fire.

*Sgt Ian John McKay, Wortley, Sheffield, 3rd Bn, Parachute Regt, for charging the enemy on Mount Longdon, Falkland Islands, in 1982; killed at the moment he extricated his comrades from a perilous situation.

Colour-Sgt Edward McKenna, Leeds, 65th Regt (late York and Lancaster), for intrepidly leading a charge after both his officers had been shot when heavily outnumbered in New Zealand in 1863.

L/Sgt Frederick McNess, Bramley, Leeds, 1st Bn, Scots Guards, for leading his men with great dash under heavy shell and machine-gun fire into enemy trenches in France in 1916, and then successfully in a counter-attack in which he was severely wounded.

2nd Lt Thomas Harold Broadbent Maufe, Ilkley, 124th Siege Battery, Royal Garrison Artillery, for repairing a telephone wire under intense artillery fire in France in 1917, and extinguishing a fire in an exploding ammunition dump.

Cpl Samuel Meekosha (later Ingham), Leeds, 1/6th Bn, West Yorkshire Regt, for taking command in an isolated trench in France in 1916, and saving at least four lives by digging out men buried by shellfire in full view of the close-range enemy.

Sgt Albert Mountain, Leeds, 15/17th Bn, West Yorkshire Regt, for attacking an enemy patrol in a critical situation in France in 1918, and, with four men, holding 600 enemy at bay for thirty minutes to cover the rest of his company's retirement and then holding a flank for twenty-seven hours until surrounded.

Sgt Andrew Moynihan, Wakefield, 90th Regt (later the Cameronians), for his valour in a storming party in the Crimea in 1855, killing five Russians and rescuing a wounded officer under heavy fire.

Sgt William Napier, Bingley, 1st Bn, 13th Regt (later Somerset Light Infantry), for rescuing a severely wounded private in India in 1858, staying with him at great risk, tending his wounds and then carrying him to safety.

Sgt John William Ormsby MM, Dewsbury, 2nd Bn, KOYLI, for showing complete indifference to enemy fire, clearing a village in France in 1918, driving out snipers and taking command when the only surviving officer was wounded, and leading his company forward.

Pte John Pearson, Leeds, 8th Hussars (later King's Royal Irish), one of a party of four VCs in India in 1858, who routed the enemy with a charge into their camp, returning with two enemy guns under heavy and converging fire.

Pte Arthur Poulter, East Witton, N Yorkshire, 1/4th Bn, Duke of Wellington's Regt, for carrying ten badly wounded men to safety on his back through heavy artillery and machine-gun fire, and then another who had been left behind, then bandaging forty men under fire before being seriously wounded attempting another rescue.

A/Sgt John Crawshaw Raynes, Eccleshall, Sheffield, 71 Brigade, Royal Field Artillery, for bandaging and carrying a wounded sergeant to a dug-out in France in 1915, and giving him his own gas helmet when gas shelling started, returning to his own gun when badly gassed, and then next day helping to extricate men buried under a shelled house before having his own wounds tended.

Cpl George Sanders MC, New Wortley, Leeds, 1/7th Bn, West Yorkshire Regt, for taking charge on the Somme in 1916, when isolated with thirty men after taking an enemy trench, and fighting off counter-attacks for thirty-six hours without food and water (which had been given to the wounded) until relieved.

Pte Albert Edward Shepherd, Royston, Barnsley, 12th (S) Bn, King's Royal Rifle Corps, for rushing (against orders) and capturing a machine gun holding up his company in France in 1917, and then, when the last officer and NCO had become casualties, leading his company to its objective.

Bosun's Mate John Sheppard CGM, Hull, Royal Navy, for twice unsuccessfully trying in great danger to blow up Russian warships in Sevastopol, Crimea, in 1855, in a punt of his own design.

*Pte William Henry Short, Eston, Teesside, 8th Bn, Yorkshire Regt, for bombing the enemy in France, 1916, although wounded, and continuing to prime bombs for others until he died after his leg was shattered by a shell.

Pte Ernest Sykes, Saddleworth, 27 (S) Bn, Northumberland Fusiliers, for bringing back four wounded at Arras, France, in 1917, under heavy fire, and then making a fifth trip in what seemed to be inviting death to bandage all too badly injured to be moved.

Sgt William Bernard Traynor, Hull, 2nd Bn, West Yorkshire Regt, for running out of a trench in South Africa in 1901 under heavy fire to help a wounded man and, though wounded himself, carrying the man with assistance to shelter and then remaining in command of his section until an attack failed.

*Pte Horace Waller, Batley Carr, 10 (S) Bn, KOYLI, for repulsing an attack in which five comrades were killed in France in 1917, by throwing bombs for an hour and then throwing bombs for thirty minutes when he remained the only unscathed member of the garrison before he, too, was killed.

Pte Charles Ward, Hunslet, Leeds, 2nd Bn, KOYLI, the last VC to be decorated by Queen Victoria, for saving his post by volunteering to take a message from his surrounded detachment in South Africa in 1900 and then returning, though wounded in the process.

T/Capt Archie Cecil Thomas White MC, Boroughbridge, 6th Bn, Yorkshire Regt, for holding a redoubt in France in 1916 for four days under heavy fire and attacks, and then saving his virtually overrun position by leading a counter-attack.

Pte Jack White, Leeds, 6th Bn, King's Own Royal Lancaster Regt, for saving his pontoon as the only uninjured man on it by towing it under heavy fire across a river in Mesopotamia in 1917, saving an officer's life, arms and equipment, and landing the wounded.

Bombardier Thomas Wilkinson, York, Royal Marine Artillery, for gallant conduct with advanced batteries at Sevastopol, Crimea, in 1855, repairing damage to defences 'under the most galling fire'.

Cpl Harry Blanshard Wood MM, Newton-on-Derwent, 2nd Bn, Scots Guards, for taking command and leading his platoon in France in 1918, lying down behind a large brick in open space and firing continuously at snipers to cover his men as they worked their way across a river, and then repelling repeated counter-attacks.

Index